Right Kingdom, Wrong Stories

Right Kingdom, Wrong Stories

A Backward Reading of Matthew's Parables

SAM TSANG

WIPF & STOCK · Eugene, Oregon

RIGHT KINGDOM, WRONG STORIES
A Backward Reading of Matthew's Parables

Wipf and Stock Publishers
199 W. 8th Ave., Suite 3
Eugene, OR 97401
www.wipfandstock.com

ISBN 13: 978-1-62564-078-9
Manufactured in the U.S.A.

Contents

Preface

WHAT IS THIS BOOK FOR?

THIS BOOK IS WRITTEN to the curious reader who finds Matthew's parables too subtle to understand. You may be a lay reader or a busy pastor. While many write homiletic books with an eye for biblical studies, I write this book as a biblical studies specialist with a homiletic eye. I hope to use simple language, leaving behind overly technical jargon and extended footnotes. I am indebted to colleagues and students alike, especially to the colleagues who wrote the blurbs and gave me advice on how to improve the manuscript. Many thanks also go to Wipf and Stock for accepting this book for publication.

WHAT IS A PARABLE?

In Jesus' world, parables were fictional stories created to make a certain point, much like modern sermon illustrations or anecdotes in speeches. I have just given the most basic definition of a parable, one I would give to a group of church-going youngsters. One element is still lacking in my definition: what a parable does. We should know both what a parable is and what a parable does in order to understand what really is a parable.

People have looked at parables variously in church history. Let me use the simplest terminology to describe the various approaches.[1] The first is the *allegorical* approach. An allegory is a story imbued with symbolic characters. In the classic story of *Pilgrim's Progress*, John Bunyan named the main character "Christian," making him the symbol of the common believer whose journey is represented in the story. Many have avoided an

---

1. For an excellent and scholarly work, see Snodgrass, *Stories with Intent*, 4–6. The entire work is a detailed and comprehensive study on parables.

allegorical approach to parables. Yet, those same opponents might see the sheep as Christians and goats as non-Christians in Matt 26:31–46, even though Jesus did not use such words to assign symbolic meaning to the two groups. Is such a meaning even possible for both Jesus and Matthew?

The second approach to parables is what I call the *one-point* approach. This has been quite popular for a long time; since the beginning of the twentieth century. The one-point approach is a move towards the opposite of the allegorical approach, suggesting that each parable has basically one point. Certainly, Jesus had made some parables quite clear about the one point he was after, often with the conclusion "therefore" (e.g., Matt 25:13). The problem with both of these views is not that they do not make any sense, but that they are extremes. Even if we read Jesus as straightforwardly as possible, some parables definitely fit into the genre of allegory. The problem is not whether Jesus could or could not use allegory and typologies but whether we should interpret a non-typological story to be full of typologies. What if Jesus never explicitly assigned symbolism to the characters in stories? The interpretation then becomes more challenging.

In this study, some of the parables will also demonstrate that there might be more than one point within a broader message. The single message is not always clear either. The meaning is often highly dependent on how we arrive at meanings. Surely, Jesus' meaning (and Matthew's meaning) is highly dependent on his audience.[2] I would add specifically that I date the Gospel in a certain time period to make it more specific to get a kind of profile of the audience, trying desperately but deliberately to step into *their* world so that the Gospel can step into *our* world. Thus, I walk a fine line between a specific audience and too general of an audience. The time period of authorship is probably best set around 70 CE. The audience probably knew the Hebrew Scriptures well enough to make sense of Matthew's writing. Other than this brief remark, my discussion of Matthew's world will elaborate more on what kind of experience these audiences had and how we also share some of the same experiences (though in different manifestations) in our world.

In recent parable studies, scholars have viewed a parable as a single point moral-theological illustration and metaphor.[3] Metaphor, the inter-

---

2. I follow Richard Bauckham's insistence that the Gospel was for all audiences because within Christian communities, information got passed around within the network relatively quick. See Bauckham, "From Whom Were Gospels Written?" For the speed of how fast travel was in traveling season, see Thompson, "The Holy Internet," 61.

3. Brosend, *Conversations with Scripture*, 5–8, gives a very simple survey. He also

pretive method of this study, is a very popular way of looking at a parable. I am not saying that a parable is the same as a metaphor, but it can function like a metaphor. Metaphor is usually a condensed analogy pointing towards a concept. For example, we may say, "The man is a pig." In the American culture, that phrase describes either a fat man or a man who behaves in a sexist manner. In Chinese culture, the same phrase can mean that the man is stupid. From my example about the pigs, we may notice two characteristics of metaphors. First, metaphors borrow one reality to point towards another reality. The pig is the sign in the metaphor, and when combined with "man," it conveys a message about the man that goes beyond the entire meaning of "pig." Second, metaphors derive their meanings from the culture in which they are found. By themselves, they can easily convey the wrong meaning. Thus, metaphors themselves, combined with cultural understanding, are the means of a message but are not the message themselves.

When we look at a parable as a metaphor (i.e., "the kingdom of God is . . ."), we are really talking about what a parable does as much as what a parable is. Like a road sign, a metaphor points towards a destination, but it is not the destination itself. It also points away from something else. When the sign points away, it often conveys a large dose of irony. Thus, any sign can function in two ways, not just one: pointing towards a destination, but at the same time pointing away from another destination. The present study will look at both what the sign points towards and points away from when Matthew portrayed Jesus' parables.[4]

---

points to allegory as a type of more ancient interpretation. Crossan, *The Power of Parable*, 1–10, also points out the metaphorical aspect of parables. He also gives subcategories of riddles, example parables, challenge parables, and so on. Such subcategorization is very helpful, but is not the main purpose of my present study.

4. I use a specific kind of language to discuss Matthew. In my simple explanation of the text, I try to talk about "what Jesus said." When I talk about Matthew's audience, I use "what Matthew's Jesus said" or "what Matthew said." I use this language not so much to question the reliability of Matthew's record, but to convey the importance of understanding Matthew as an interpreter, translator, and theologian of Jesus' original message. After all, if Jesus spoke mostly Aramaic, as most of the New Testament scholars have indicated, Matthew had to translate Jesus into Greek. The act of translation is creative as well as interpretive.

WHAT IF THE PARABLE GETS TURNED UPSIDE DOWN?

There are two sides to every story, so the popular saying goes. Yet, when we read Jesus' parables, we often only read one side. Why not both? What if we stick by the old adage and look at both sides of the story instead of one?

Jesus' parables are fascinating in that they tell of a world in a faraway place with quite different values. Generations have been inspired by Jesus' parables. From the many scholarly readings of the parables, we cannot deny that parables stir the imagination. The puzzle remains whether we can decipher what values Jesus was railing against as much as what Jesus stood for. The rhetoric of Jesus within each Gospel writers' framework deserves a bit of reflection.

Jesus is known for one thing among many scholars; he was a revolutionary thinker. He was not the type that would overturn empires by violence, but his teaching was not merely that of a prototypical Jewish man of his time. As a peaceful preacher and miracle worker, he died the death of a rebel. He also commented on his society and reversed the values that he saw as harmful. Sometimes, he reversed the convention in order for listeners to choose between his kingdom value and the world's value. Other times, he stuck with certain kind of convention when he saw the opposition taking a deviant convention, again forcing a choice upon his listeners. As a result of Jesus' creative genius, instead of dissolving tension, Jesus often created tension. What if we take that paradigm and run with it? What if we tell some of Jesus' parables backwards or in a modified manner that dissolves all the tension in order to see the issues in a clearer manner?[5] What if each story has a mirror and opposite image? What if each story contains two stories instead of one?

---

5. Mikhail Bakhtin is greatly helpful in looking at the upside down world of Jesus even though he passed in 1975. His concept of carnival, expounded largely in his classic *Rabelais and His World*, is a great model in understanding the parable. The concept basically comes from the way people behave in a carnival festival. Their behavior is far from normal and in many ways countercultural. In other words, they simply can't behave in such a manner and still live life from day to day. See also Bakhtin, *The Dialogic Imagination*, 71. Within the carnival, cultural concepts become the butt of humor and mockery. Bakhtin's observation has gone a long way to give a metanarrative to many cultures where this carnivalesque element exists. The Saturnalia of the ancient Roman culture comes to mind. The modern Mardi Gras in New Orleans or the Brazilian Carnival also have such elements. What does all this have to do with Jesus' parables? A lot! The reading of the parables in this book will tell Jesus' parables backwards based on what normally would have happened according to Jesus' societal values, in order to show how Jesus reversed such values as a criticism.

In both our ecclesiastical and academic communities alike, many have written wonderfully on the parables using historical, cultural, and literary approaches. In this book, I wish to focus on the literary dimension of parables by noting the plot (composed of the main problem, the response of the various characters, and Jesus' conclusion) before looking at what such a story meant to Matthew's audience. They too had to make a choice, facing a different set of challenges than Jesus' original audience.

My goal is to make the literary reading accessible to the average reader. In Jesus' conclusion, he would give hints to the hinges of a parable's plot. The hinges were where the storyteller could tell the story in all different ways. By looking at the alternative way Jesus could have told a story, we will also find out what concept Jesus was pointing away from. Thus, a metaphor in story form, a parable, does not only point towards a message but also points away from its opposite. Most readers of parables tend to see only one side of the story, but in reality, there are two sides to each story, forcing readers to choose. The flip side of a parable can be just as informative as the parable itself. The place where Jesus' story can go one way or the opposite way is probably where the parable exerts the sharpest metaphorical force. I will use my Asian-American experience to shed light on many cultural dimensions of that ancient world.

Why do we need to do both sides of the story? When told upside down, we can explore how telling the parable another way would impact Matthew's audience and their choice to live their lives differently. Indeed many in the modern faith community are unconsciously living the backward story, dissolving all the tension Jesus' ministry had created back in his day and ours. It is important to look at the backward way so that modern Christ followers can become aware. By living the opposite value from Jesus', modern believers (as well as ancient ones) actually become unfaithful to Jesus' kingdom message. Therefore, I shall take the following steps in reading these parables, concluding with probing questions on how such a reading implicates the text and modern life. In a sense, this is a kind of Bible study as a result of a careful literary reading. Hopefully, this humble work will help all those who are interested in Jesus' parables, whether they are preachers or lay Bible readers, Christians or non-Christians.

METHOD OF READING

The readership of my book should be quite wide but many preachers will find help in this book because of its partially homiletical aim of giving imaginative readings of parables for sermons. For the non-preachers who just enjoy the Bible for their faith (or for anything else), the backward re-telling will take them away from years of flat Bible reading into a more imaginative first-century world.

For starters, I shall start with a little survey on the background of Matthew and his audience. This is not a New Testament introduction. I shall not belabor the pros and cons of this and that on authorship dates. I however need to give a methodological perspective from which the reading will take place. So, my creation of a hypothetical background from which Matthew wrote his work is important. In this creation, I will try to simplify issues by using modern illustrations from mainstream American culture as well as my experience teaching overseas as an ethnic Chinese, and as an Asian-American in the US. Surprisingly, many such illustrations show that we are closer today to Matthew's situation than many originally thought.

Following a brief survey of the world of Matthew (just enough for the purpose of our reading), I shall reconstruct a backward reading of Jesus' parable. For my readers who are looking for ways to structure their sermons, the backward reading is greatly helpful to show the real problem in a "problem-solution" format of a sermon. Many narratives (and parables are narratives) are conducive to the problem-solution formula. Not all the parables can fit into a backward reading paradigm, but the majority can. Based on the backgrounds of Jesus and Matthew, the plot line of many of the parables can be told all different ways. Sometimes, I would take out some important elements and notice the consequence of such a reading. Especially due to the fact that different characters in the parable could react differently in the society, we must never assume that Jesus' parables are predictable, straightforward, and single-directional. I must then entertain different possible scenarios of how people would see themselves in these fictional stories (parables are fictional stories) when listening to Jesus and being drawn into Jesus' narrative world. Some of the wording will be based on one translation of the Bible, the New English Translation (NET).[6] I shall reverse the key elements in the parable to stimulate my reader's imagina-

---

6. For an online version, please see www.bible.org. The printed version of this excellent study Bible also contains quite helpful exegetical information for all students of the Bible.

tion of how the parable could have been told. If we are preachers, this is where we can stir the imagination of our listeners and can draw them into Jesus' fictional world. My basis for retelling the parable is, of course, based on Jesus' interpretation of his own parable. I shall read each parable the way narratives should be read, based on origin and location of the narrative, the character responses, and Jesus' final conclusion about the story. During this imaginative backward telling of the story, my readers will notice a repeated conclusion to each backward telling of the story the sentence, "Yet, neither Jesus nor Matthew told the story this way." I wanted to emphasize this alternative backward telling to show the other side of how a story could have been told, but was not. This is to show some of the opposite values both Jesus and Matthew addressed.

After the backward (and quite often, shocking) reading of each parable, I shall provide the discussion of the key elements of the backward story plot, followed by looking at the way Jesus really told the parable. This discussion is important to highlight the story world of Jesus. Within this discussion, I will look at the broader context of the parable by looking at the surrounding contexts for clues to why Jesus told it, to whom Jesus told the story, and how the parable impacts the entire book narrative. In doing so, we frame the small narrative of the parable within the larger narrative of the book.

Before I talk about preaching, I shall look at the implications of the meaning for the world of Matthew and his readers and ours. This is where I answer the question, "What does the parable have to do with making me a better Christian or making the church a better community?" After discussing the significance of parables for ancient and modern readers, I shall include suggestions on preaching and studying these parables for those who struggle with them in their pulpit or Bible studies. For preachers, I would advocate an imaginative reading of such stories not only to know what values they advocate, but also what values they downgrade. Both are important in thoughtful preaching. Then, preachers should invite the listener to make a choice for the kingdom. Finally, I end each parable with a set of questions to think about for modern times.

This is not primarily an academic book even though it has an academic backbone. Rather, it is a purely literary experiment and an exercise of the imagination that takes seriously Jesus' role as an innovator and reformer of cultural convention in his teaching about the kingdom. I shall therefore skip any footnote unless it is absolutely necessary. There are many fine academic works that will discuss the background, sources, and the grammatical intricacies of these parables. Such is not the goal of this simple offering. Obviously, my way is one man's reading in the ocean of readings of Jesus' parables. At the very least, I hope my discussion will start some kind of conversation about parables beyond either the weighty academic exploration of sources or the simplistic straightforward ecclesiastical applications. What if each story contains two sides instead of one? My study will show a richer reading when we read with both sides of the story in mind.

Introduction to Reading Matthew's Parables

Matthew's World

A TIME OF CHAOS

MATTHEW'S WORLD WAS CHAOTIC. Some scholars date Matthew before 70 CE, but most do not. Matthew probably wrote his work after the great destruction of Jerusalem, a tragic event in Jewish history. The Jewish war, or the great Jewish revolt, dated around 66–70 CE. In reality, many smaller uprisings had flared up before this gigantic explosion. Judas the Galilean had already revolted against the Romans on taxation issues around 6 CE. Of course, he was not successful. If Josephus's account of the tension and complications in Galilee reflects reality, then the Jewish revolt was a foregone conclusion with many preceding mini-conflicts.

According to Josephus, the Jewish historian and a contemporary of Paul, the Jews fought not only the Romans but also among themselves. The best example came from Galilee where Jesus did most of his ministry. Galilee was far from a happy place. According to the histories of that time, Galilee was populated with Jews who struggled against Roman colonial control. The Romans had a tough time dealing with the unhappy sentiments among Galileans. Josephus's portrait shows that Galilee was largely Jewish with a colonizing gentile veneer. Scholarly consensus has largely confirmed this general portrait.

The Galilean picture Josephus painted looks a bit like pre-World-War-II China, where warlords fought for control over populations and territories. Josephus also showed that different cities had their own self-interest. In his (probably quite accurate) self-portrait, Josephus was a prominent leader trying to keep the factions from killing each other and killing him. What caused such a scenario? The Romans often favored and developed certain cities to promote their imperial propaganda. Thus, many different cities in Galilee vied for the support of Rome. When Rome did not support them, they turned on Rome and those other favored cities. Internal conflicts would ensue among the pro-Roman and anti-Roman factions. These cities were not highly populated like the urban centers of today. Sometimes only around 10,000 citizens populated a relatively large city. If they want to muster up forces against the Romans, they were simply no match for the Romans.

By the end of the Jewish war, all the revolutionary factions had been crushed. The Jewish war that lasted more than three years testified to the powerful militia forces of Judaism. At the same time, these forces were no longer able to defend Jewish interests or even local interests. In some ways, Judaism has never been the same since the 70-CE destruction. How could it? Formerly, the religion centered on the temple. After 70 CE, the central location of Judaism had been forever destroyed. During this period, many were losing hope in this world. A certain literary genre called apocalyptic literature became very popular, pointing to a heavenly reality that would eventually overcome the evil of this world. In such literature, one repeated theme is the election of God's people.

Another large group that survived well into formative Judaism after 70 CE was the Pharisees. As they became the powerful group, they probably got into some conflicts with Jesus' followers or vice versa. As we read Matthew, we should note that the early church was a part of Judaism and not apart from it. Many believers were still tied to the temple or the synagogue system. With the temple destruction, many would be quite confused as to how they would respond now. Their belief that Jesus was the messiah might also cause problems for them with synagogues, gatherings inside a "house of prayer." Probably the worst-case scenario would be alienation from the synagogue. Different groups also struggled with who was the rightful interpreter of the law. When the powerful leaders kicked out some of Jesus' followers, the latter experienced separation from their own culture and connections. These were challenging times indeed. Matthew's audience was therefore struggling with whether or not they were the elect community.

RELATIONAL TRANSACTION

Besides power struggles between different factions, Matthew's world was also a place for power struggle between people. It is common for scholars to say that Matthew worked within the system of "patron-client" or "honor and shame," but what do these terms mean to non-technical readers? Matthew's society finds many parallels with modern cultures. Let me illustrate.

In my own ethnic culture, the Chinese culture, there are certain unspoken rules in relationships. When people within the family are in need, we are obligated to help them. People with higher ranks often pay for the meals of the ones in the lower rank—but not in a straightforward way, rather by having a ritual of fighting for the check that eventually is paid by the person with the highest social ranking and financial means. For such financial and social patronage, loyalty is expected in return. When people give us gifts, we always try to reciprocate as a show of gratitude. A failure to reciprocate would be considered bad form. The shame of such discourtesy would put a person in bad standing in the community.

In Matthew's world, the idea of appropriate exchange was also a social force. In principle, such exchange is beneficial because it forces participants to maintain civil relationships with one another without neglecting to show gratitude. The trouble with such exchange is the equality of the gifts. For a millionaire, giving a brand-name watch would mean very little. If the recipient makes minimum wage, giving back equally to the rich giver would be impossible. Now the millionaire would probably not expect gift of equal value, but the shame of giving too cheaply would always cause shame for the poorer recipient, putting the recipient in a subordinate position. The poorer recipient would always become the less dignified party.

In mainstream American culture, relationships can also be a matter of benefits and exchanges. These days, in business success seminars, gurus teach us that it is important to keep our network broad in order to succeed. "Professional success" becomes the main reason to build relationships. Relationship is just one more tool we can use to obtain our end. We can "use" relationship. Relationship can easily becomes the means to an end rather than the end. In Matthew's society, relationships with power people were indeed important for those who wanted to succeed in life. Of course, it is unfair for us to judge them by saying that they were being selfish because millions of Americans do exactly that with almost every one of their relationships. The phrase "It is not what you know but whom you know that matters" perfectly describes such relationships.

In Asian culture, the elders receive ascribed authority by default. The more traditional the culture is, the greater deference people pay to the elderly. The presupposition behind such ascribed honor is the cumulative wisdom of an elder. If taken to extremes, the young will never question the older member of the household. Matthew's world also had ascribed honor for those people whose authority was given by the society. Such honorees received power and privileges not accessible to ordinary people. Their powers often went unchecked.

Since I have lived in both Asia and the US, I have noticed the hyper-competitiveness of my fellow Americans. In other societies where polite relationships become the glue of society, winning an argument is less important than harmonious relationships. Not so with many Americans. Some people would go to great lengths to win in all sorts of arenas, including arguments with someone, as personal honor is at stake. Losing is not the American way. Most of my Asian examples above show ascribed honor. In this mainstream American example, I have shown achieved honor. The same fact of life also impacted Matthew's world. In such a world, people who won in contests would rise in rank. People did not easily back down because of the personal honor at stake.

From this above picture, Matthew's world starts with grace, courtesy, and honor but people often turned relationship into a transaction. This would be truer for commoners. Since Matthew's world was mostly made up of commoners, they would know precisely such dynamics. They would operate by such relational rules of transaction. Both ascribed and achieved honor also existed. Although at first glance Matthew's world is quite foreign to ours, the above examples show that many traits do appear in the modern world. These traits are human attributes, not limited to the ancient world of Matthew. They only manifest differently in different times and cultures.

CORPORATE PERSONALITY

Matthew's world, indeed the early Christian world, was a place where corporate personality took precedent over individual interest. I am not suggesting that people were not concerned with personal interests, but they tended to look at how others around them behaved, and lived accordingly. Similar approaches can be found in the modern world.

I recall going to a soccer game in England where the fan culture is especially illustrative of the corporate personality. My friend (who was a fan of the visitors) brought me to a match of the local team. Out of the kindness of his heart, we sat in the home fan section. When his team scored, he could not stand up and cheer. In fact, he had to wear his own team's jersey underneath his sweater. To make matters worse, some visiting fans could not control themselves. Instead of hiding their identity like my friend, they stood up and cheered for the visiting team. The police quickly escorted them to the visiting fan section for their own protection and to maintain the overall law and order. Certain behavior is expected in a certain section of seating in the English game. Contrary behavior would invite strange glances at best and physical violence at worst.

In my own Chinese culture, one example of corporate personality stands out especially. In many big aristocratic families, the so-called old-money crowd, members keep a hierarchy by using the middle character of the three characters of the Chinese name. Every generation changes the middle character to show where each generation fits. Each family is tied to the greater family with the same surname. Every single person knows where s/he is in the whole scheme of things. Those who are higher up on the ladder would immediately receive honor without having to earn it. Not many within such traditional families question such practice. This is still true in some cases today. The group identity dominates the individual interest. Each individual behaves according to the group identity.

A further illustration from my own ethnic group also aptly illustrates how corporate personality actually works. Within the Chinese culture, fictive kinship is important. Even within certain American cultures, this also applies. We call our parents' friends "uncles" and our grandparents' friends "grandpas" and "grandmas." In the way we use the family metaphor, the entire Chinese race is one gigantic family well testified by our interaction.

This corporate personality also influences religion in no small manner in both Judaism and the modern Chinese church. The parallel example of the modern Chinese church illustrates adequately the issue facing Matthew. One of the problems of the Chinese church culture is mission. To put it very bluntly, most Chinese churches do "mission" to their own people, even if they move to a different country, they still try to reach other Chinese migrants. Part of the reason is due to cultural identity from 5,000 years of history. Furthermore, as the most populated people group, the Chinese are just all over the world. Thus, even in Christian ministry that touts a proselytizing focus, this strong cultural identity mostly prevents a cross-cultural campaign. Illustrations from my own culture here will benefit the reading of Matthew.

Matthew's heavy concern for many things Jewish without any detailed explanation can only lead us to conclude that his audience was primarily Jewish or at least quite familiar with Judaism. In Matthew's world, a certain group is expected to behave a certain way. Quite often, people would try to legitimate their behavior from the ancient laws, such as the Torah. The importance of Sabbath keeping was no news for any average Judean in the first century. An average Judean would eat kosher without a second thought. Why indeed would diet be important other than for Torah observation? It is because kinship was often expressed with extended family meals. This is typical of many cultures. The Americans have their Thanksgiving meal. The Chinese have their New Year meals. Such behavior was more than mere religion, because religiosity varied in degree. Of course, this is not to say that it was always possible to behave according to the corporate personality. Some would knowingly rebel while others would inadvertently deviate from the norm. However, if deviance occurred, consequences would follow. Following the status quo usually brought honor and praise. Deviance posed great risk. Those who committed the deviance would have to justify their behavior by claiming greater accuracy in interpretation of the Torah and tracing more ancient roots from the forefathers. We will see that Jesus sometimes deviated from the norm in our study of the parables. In fact, we need to notice such deviance. Matthew's writing goes some way in defending Jesus' honor while pointing out the necessary deviance.

One deviance from the corporate personality in Matthew's community is mission. With some of the Jesus' followers being kicked out of synagogues, how would they form their group identity? One way to do so was to mix in with gentile society. The choice was clear. My illustration from my own culture shows the difficulty of doing so because of strong ethnic history. For the Jewish believers in Matthew's congregation, the difficulty doubled because their original ethnicity was identified with religion. Their former biological fictive family (i.e., being the children of Abraham) now would slowly form a new fictive family that included gentile "brothers and sisters." At the same time, somehow, this new fictive family had to be tied back to the Hebrew Bible tradition of their former fictive family. The new norm would be a different continuity of the old norm. Matthew's audience would have to face a new challenge because they would have to violate many of their basic practices such as purity rituals. They would eventually have to adjust their association and habits when in gentile company.

IDENTITY CRISIS

Besides the internal struggle between those who thought Jesus was lord and those who thought otherwise, Jews who went into the post-70 CE diaspora also faced a serious identity crisis. Colonization was never a happy occasion, but this latest episode in 70 CE added insult to injury and salt in the wound.

Obviously, to someone like Josephus, rebel turned Roman historian, who received much benefit from the Romans, the Roman occupation could be thought of as the lesser of many evils. Not everyone was as lucky as Josephus. Those who lost relatives in the war would hold horrible bitterness. Those who valued their spiritual experience of pilgrimage to Jerusalem would find the loss of the temple a bitter pill to swallow. How then could anyone function after this blatant colonial pillage of the most important cultural-religious architecture called the temple?

The above discussion about integration with gentiles should be read with Roman occupation in mind. It is a very difficult situation to assess. At the most basic level, how do you treat an enemy and occupying force? Matthew's community faced this problem as Christ-followers, and not merely as enthusiasts of nationalism. We can simply dismiss people like Josephus as sell-outs to their own race, but reality was far more complex. If we read the rhetoric of Josephus, we will find him citing historical situation of Daniel and other prophets as examples of divine control. Of course, others would have different convictions of not seeing divine control in such a horrible event. The stories in Matthew are also capable of different levels of discourse as well, moving this way and that at different junctures. Modern readers should be quite aware of the different levels, especially those in the faith community.

Matthew's audience had different convictions about how to interpret the colonial power that was over them. Any occupied people group, especially faith communities, would be concerned with the difficulty of appropriating such events. For example, in Egypt, after the Arab Spring, many Christians, Coptic or otherwise, felt the tension as they perceived their rights being taken away. While the West celebrated initially with the overturning of Mubarak's government, the situation quickly deteriorated. Hardline Muslims had destroyed many churches and committed grave violence against fellow Egyptian citizens. Without going into the complexity, I have had different interactions with Egyptian Christians from different denominations. Some swore that they would protest and take it to the streets with the same enthusiasm as they did with the Arab Spring movement. Others chose to sit back and wait. They knew their identity as Egyptian Christians, but their concern over a possible Muslim occupation put them in a peculiar place. Would taking to the streets in active resistance or sitting back to watch be the best tact? Is there any space in the faith proposed by Matthew for resistance towards such occupation? The community of Jesus' followers has had to face that issue more than once. These issues would be part of their identity formation, in this time of uncertainty for Matthew's audience. Central to this identity would be God's role in history and in the community. Resistance did not need to take the form of armed revolt. Writing could well be a kind of literary resistance against Rome. The most blatant effort was the book of Revelation by John the Seer. Would Matthew have the resistive space for present reading?

In much of postcolonial literature, resistance came in the form of coded writing against Rome with subtle mockery and satire. If we read Matthew's parables through a postcolonial perspective (assuming my reconstruction is right), we may discover a new awareness of literary resistance, or the absence of it, in Matthew's writing. Whether Matthew was in favor of or against resistance, he had to face the issue. The community would form its identity from and not apart from this experience. Could God be the character in the story that could be used to mock the colonists as James McLaren's Josephus had done?[1] The questions are intriguing and must not be dismissed for their impact on identity formation. Horizontally, this group would have to see the ruling gentiles in a certain light based on Matthew's narrative world. At the top level and vertically (i.e., interacting with superior powers), perhaps they had to interact with the policies and even the policymakers whose decisions would continue to impact the group identity. Was the interaction of Jesus and his disciples with governing authorities a Matthean model for his community? This too is an intriguing question that deserves some reflection.

The above challenge can be seen in a place where I used to teach full-time. I shall use Hong Kong to close this discussion about identity formation. Many in Hong Kong had been colonized by Britain. With China taking over 1997, hopes were high about China's possible positive influence. That hope has waned. Now many have called China's policy as part of the new occupation or neo-colonialism. As a result, people often come

---

1. McLaren, "A Reluctant Provincial," 44.

out several times a year to protest freedom-restrictive policies and other injustices. What was the church's response?

The church's response (if she responds at all) comes in two forms. First, several of the mainline churches speak out against unjust governmental policies. Second, a number of churches (especially quite a few megachurches) speak in favor of patience with governmental policies. Both sides present many vigorous points arguing in favor of their positions. Running a middle ground would be the Baptists who valued individual conscience and conviction in dealing with political issues. While most people would never consider themselves British, many would not consider themselves "Chinese" either. For them, "Chinese" has the connotation of being associated with oppressive mainland government.[2] Most consider themselves Hong Kongers. This unique phenomenon also affects the way the church reacts to the situation. Those who react against the government continue to decry the bad witness of those who advocate patience. The society has a very large and vocal population that opposes mainland control via the Hong Kong government. By speaking out, many churches consider themselves standing on the side of justice and the oppressed, thus creating a strong and visible witness as Christian Hong Kongers. Those who advocate patience (and even sometimes giving in wholesale) with government often accuse the opposition of being reactionary, and quite capable of committing frequent verbal violence. Some who advocate patience see this harmonious approach with the government as the way to earn their right to spread the gospel in the mainland. In many ways, they would firmly consider themselves "Chinese." The tension then, as a Christian, is between the "Hong Konger" Christians and "Chinese" Christians (much like the Confessing Church and the German Christians).

As we can see from all these narratives above, any kind of political upheaval will cause the church to reflect on her identity. This reflection was no different for the faith community of Matthew's time. There was no escape from dealing with political forces inside and outside the faith community. Neither is there any escape today. Matthew's situation has its own message even to the modern reader.

---

2. Most Hong Kongers will consider themselves "Han-Chinese," to be precise. "Han" is a people group that ruled the other people groups in China. Some do not use "Chinese" any more due to its connection with the mainland.

1

An Easy Harvest?

On that day after Jesus went out of the house, he sat by the lake. And such a large crowd gathered around him that he got into a boat to sit while the whole crowd stood on the shore. He told them this story: "Listen! A farmer wanted to sow some seeds. Before he sowed, he had decided to use his oxen to till the soil and clear the land. In his clearing, he ripped up the soil so that the seed would land in the soil. He took away the rocks that would block the seeds and ripped up the thorns that would stop the seeds from going in. Finally, he had created the ideal soil before he sowed. The soil then sprang forth crop, some more and some less: a hundred, sixty, or thirty times what was sown. The one who has ears had better listen!

So listen to the parable of the sower: When anyone hears the word about the kingdom and does not understand it, the evil one comes and snatches. This is why the sower had to rip up the soil to keep seeds in the ground. As we all know, rocks can keep the seed from taking root. If a man has no root in himself and does not endure; when trouble or persecution comes because of the word, immediately he falls away. Therefore, the sower had to take away rocks in his clearing the land. Other problems could occur. Worldly cares and the seductiveness of wealth, like thorns, could choke the word, so it produces nothing. The sower also ripped up the thorns. After all the preparation, the soil had become acceptable and friendly ground for the seed. The friendly ground is the person who hears the word and understands. He bears fruit, yielding a hundred, sixty, or thirty times what was sown."

I GREW UP IN the South and the Midwest US. In rural areas, there is no shortage of farming equipment. Most farmers invest in farming equipment. One of the most important pieces of equipment is the chisel plow. The plow can break up stubborn ground and cover a large area. This piece of equipment breaks up the soil to get it ready for planting so that no seed planted was lost. Farmers would further drag a disc harrow, a kind of rotating disc blades, with a tractor to grind up the soil so that the seeds would be assured a good resting and growing place. Without such equipment, bad harvest, bankruptcy, and possible starvation await the farmer.

In this retelling of Matt 13:1–23, I have chosen to take out 13:10–17 and retell the parable in a more productive way of sowing (or farming). Sensible farmers would do all the above procedures to ensure that they would maximize their profit. Plowing, after all, was a practice in Jesus' day (Luke 9:62). Not one seed should be wasted, if possible at all. If all the preparation work was done right, the sower would reap a good harvest with very few obstacles. If the kingdom was spreading this easily, everything would be quite fine and Jesus' movement would have an easily paved road on which to follow. Both the audiences of Jesus and Matthew could choose a better-planned path, but neither Jesus nor Matthew told the story in this backward fashion.

TELLING IT NORMAL: KEY ELEMENTS IN THE STORY

On that day after Jesus went out of the house, he sat by the lake. 2 And such a large crowd gathered around him that he got into a boat to sit while the whole crowd stood on the shore. 3 He told them many things in parables, saying: "Listen! A sower went out to sow. 4 And as he sowed, some seeds fell along the path, and the birds came and devoured them. 5 Other seeds fell on rocky ground where they did not have much soil. They sprang up quickly because the soil was not deep. 6 But when the sun came up, they were scorched, and because they did not have sufficient root, they withered. 7 Other seeds fell among the thorns, and they grew up and choked them. 8 But other seeds fell on good soil and produced grain, some a hundred times as much, some sixty, and some thirty. 9 The one who has ears had better listen!"

10 Then the disciples came to him and said, "Why do you speak to them in parables?" 11 He replied, "You have been given the opportunity to know the secrets of the kingdom of heaven, but they have not. 12 For whoever has will be given more, and will have an abundance. But whoever does not have, even what he has will be taken from him. 13 For this reason I speak to them in parables: Although they see they do not see, and although they hear they do not hear nor do they understand. 14 And concerning them the prophecy of Isaiah is fulfilled that says: 'You will listen carefully yet will never understand, you will look closely yet will never comprehend.

15 'For the heart of this people has become dull; they are hard of hearing, and they have shut their eyes, so that they would not see with their eyes and hear with their ears and understand with their hearts and turn, and I would heal them.' 16 "But your eyes are blessed because they see, and your ears because they hear. 17 For I tell you the truth, many prophets and righteous people longed to see what you see but did not see it, and to hear what you hear but did not hear it.

18 "So listen to the parable of the sower: 19 When anyone hears the word about the kingdom and does not understand it, the evil one comes and snatches what was sown in his heart; this is the seed sown along the path. 20 The seed sown on rocky ground is the person who hears the word and immediately receives it with joy. 21 But he has no root in himself and does not endure; when trouble or persecution comes because of the word, immediately he falls away. 22 The seed sown among thorns is the person who hears the word, but worldly cares and the seductiveness of wealth choke the word, so it produces nothing. 23 But as for the seed sown on good soil, this is the person who hears the word and understands. He bears fruit, yielding a hundred, sixty, or thirty times what was sown."

Jesus told this parable by the lake to a large crowd (13:1). Matthew 13 contains a series of parables that deserve explanation in subsequent chapters. For now, Jesus told this series of parables starting with the sower's story. The occasion is linked with 12:46–50 because Matthew described "on that day" in 13:1. The context then was about doing the Father's will in 12:50 in a kingdom-new household.

Jesus' parable was simple and straightforward, talking about four kinds of soil: on the path, rocky places of shallow soil, thorns, and good soil. The complex part came not from the explanation but from the switch of audience in 13:10ff. The explanation of the parable, not the parable itself, only aimed at the disciples. The crowd had no role in understanding the parable, evident in "not to them" (13:11). The switch of audience appears to be a deliberate reenactment of the parable, with the kingdom secrets only given to the select few while the word was proclaimed among all.

Jesus' explanation for this switch seems to have come out of the Old Testament (13:13–15), directly from Isa 6:9, 10. Yet, the eyes and ears metaphors in Isaiah 6 come straight out of Deuteronomy 29:4 where seeing and listening would result in doing. Already, Matthew 11.25-26 correlated well with the sower parable and Isaiah 6 in keeping the kingdom mysteries from certain people. In other words, Jesus was using covenantal tradition of Isaiah 6 that went as far back as the original Torah to describe the present situation. The present situation did not look good. Isaiah 6 contains the context of Isaiah's predetermined failure. No one would listen to Isaiah as only few would go into exile. Given the fact that people memorized the Bible by passages rather than merely a verse here or there, Jesus' quotation of Isaiah 6 presumes not just a hearing but an understanding of Isaiah's context. The knowledge of the kingdom was an impossible mission. The listeners were not going to do whatever God wanted them to do. As if to make sure the entire event would go according to the predetermined result of Isaiah 6, Jesus mockingly said, "The one who has ears had better listen" in Matt 13:9, but immediately said that they would hear but not hear or understand (13:13). Matthew's portrait of the setting emphasizes the big crowd around Jesus (13:1–2). In other words, most were not going to understand or do what God wanted them to do.

Jesus then pronounced a beatitude in 13:16–17 before he revealed the secret of the sower story in 13:18–23. Jesus' discussion about Isaiah 6 came before the explanation. In other words, the fulfilled prophecy of Isaiah 6 preceded the explanation. Jesus' separation from the crowd was the deliberate fulfillment, not just by word but by action. Now, he would talk to the select group. This is the group that would see, hear, and understand according to 13:14–15. In other words, the parable was the flip side of not seeing, hearing, and understanding. Jesus' action and quotation of Isaiah matched perfectly the way the parable would develop.

The disciples saw what happened when Jesus separated from the crowd. They then were told the meaning of the parable. So, they heard and then understood. Jesus explained the parable simply in four different situations. When viewing the oral performance of Jesus (by Matthew), the interpreter ought to ask, "What would strike the original listening disciples about this whole speech?" With the repetition of seeing, hearing, and understanding in 13:13–14, the turning point of 13:16–17 not only encourages, but the encouragement has a theological, indeed eschatological, substance supporting it. The exclamation of "but *your* eyes" in 13:16 must have gotten the elect disciples' attention. *They* had seeing eyes, hearing ears and understanding heart as a result of the parable being explained.

First, the path represents the one who did not understand the word, and had the word snatched away from the heart (13:19). Second, the rocky soil represents the one who did not take root because of persecution. Third, the thorny soil represents the one who was so preoccupied with worries of this life and deceitful wealth that the word was choked out. Fourth, the good soil represents the one who would hear, understand, and bear a harvest.

When looking at the parable, it is quite easy to read the story on its own merit, even on Jesus' explanation. From the picture created by the parable, it seems that the sower was randomly wasting seed, without consideration of the soil at all. I suppose we can easily say that people back in Jesus' day just spread seed wherever they could on the land they owned. Such could not have been the case. In Jesus' day, farming involved oxen tilling the soil (Luke 9:62). Surely, the parable shows the worst way to spread the seed. In fact, Jesus' way of sowing was wasteful and stupid. The farmer had essentially taken the least profitable route. Why not just rip out the soil and get rid of all pesky things? There is no answer as to why the sower did not do that. He just did not. What can be gathered by reading the parable on its own merit?

The parable itself does not say that the sower is God. The sower could have been anyone who had the word, whether he was Isaiah or Jesus or anyone else. Jesus focused more on the word and its recipients, thus typifying something that just happened when the word went out. In fact, the only clearly identified elements in the parable are the message of the kingdom/word (13:19, 20), the evil one (13:19), and the person who heard (13.20). In this way, this parable is close to being an allegory. The climax of harvest provides a bit of good news in spite of largely bad news of wasted sowing. This parable seems more descriptive than prescriptive, as it describes what happened when the kingdom message was sent but not prescribes what one ought to do in spreading it (i.e., "Choose the right soil!"). Most of the soil was bad anyway. The parable also does not focus on the issue of "who is saved and who is not saved?" though many modern interpreters would want to speculate. It purely describes what happens with the recipients of the word. The parable then is quite limited in its meaning when read by itself. Since it is part of the speech Jesus gave leading up to the parable, interpretation cannot be complete without considering 13:11–17.[1]

The section of 13.11–17 precedes the parable, and for good reason. It serves as the underlying presupposition for reading the parable. The quotation of Isaiah is a great transition to describe what happened when Jesus separated the disciples from the crowd and what happened in the parable. Isaiah's prophecy was quite prominent in the time of Jesus and before, so much so that it became one of the most quoted (if not the most quoted) Old Testament books in the New Testament. Its plot is very much based on God's curse on those who did not obey and follow his way, resulting in the ultimate exile of the guilty. Isa 6:9–10, verses quoted by Jesus here, remained important for understanding Isaiah's own call and mission. Given the fact that Isaiah is quoted extensively in Matthew (1:23; 3:3; 4:15–16; 8:17; 12:18–20; 15:8–9; 21:13; etc.), interpreters must assume that Matthew's audience was familiar with the overall storyline of Isaiah. Jesus' explanation of Isaiah 6 as an analogy of what he was doing would make great sense both to Jesus' audience and Matthew's.

The storyline of Isa 6:9–10 talks of a people who were destined to face the exile. If Isaiah 6 is the call for Isaiah, then the section Isa 6:9–10 becomes the first prediction about Isaiah's failed mission. This unenlightened lot would not receive any enlightenment even from Isaiah's ministry and would reap their consequence. Isaiah was destined to be effective only with a small remnant. If Matthew linked Isaiah as part of the kingdom story, then even if God was in charge (i.e., kingdom of heaven), exile still could happen because God was faithful to his warnings.

If we take the storyline of Isaiah, especially in light of the gloomy announcement of Isa 6:9–10, and superimpose that storyline on Matt 13:1–17, we will discover that Jesus' work here mirrored Isaiah's. The crowd was much like what Jesus described. They did not have much but would have everything taken away from them (13:12). Just like Isaiah, Jesus was also

---

1. The seeds in 13:4 in the parable are in plural form in Greek. The indicator is the plural pronoun for what was sown. The singular is used in 13:5ff just to show perhaps Matthew's struggle to translate what is natural versus what it is that Jesus was trying to teach. The passage of Mark 4:1–9 probably shows the original saying in the singular. The seed in Matt 13:18–23 from Jesus' explanation is singular. The indicator is the singular pronoun for what was sown.

the Lord's servant. Both were going on an apparently hopeless mission that would result in rejection. Both were speaking to a remnant. Jesus' action in Matt 13:1–17 dramatized Isaiah's mission. Jesus never meant for Matt 13:1–9 to be understood by the crowd at all. The action was just part of his dramatization of the Isaiah storyline.

If we were to combine the storyline of Isaiah with Matthew's storyline here, it would look something like this. The crowd that did not see, hear, and understand behaved much like the motley crew of Isaiah. They were virtually living in preparation for the exile. The disciples were the ones who understood because Jesus selected them as the remnant out of which God would bring his new people. Thus, the sower parable was the explanation for the mission of the disciples, while Isaiah 6 was primarily an explanation of Jesus' mission. Jesus' mission here was an eschatological moment (13:17). This significant teaching moment was God's salvation history being made visible to Jesus' disciples. The disciples carried on their backs the eschatological hope of the kingdom message, the word. They would sow in the long line of sowers from Isaiah to Jesus. However, with that hope, obstacles such as the evil one, trouble, persecution, worries of life, and deceitfulness of wealth would stand in the way of the word getting to the recipients' hearts. These hearts were typical of the kinds of people (and not just a single person) who heard the word, evident in the different degrees of harvest at 13:8, 23. Jesus' parable shows Jesus to be a realist. Life of the kingdom mission would not be easy. Nevertheless, like Isaiah's case, restoration of Israel was possible through the remnant. The negatives were temporary setbacks for a brighter tomorrow, at least for Matthew's audience. Some soil would bear harvest after all. Even when God was in charge in Jesus' world, the harvest was not always predictable or global.

There is one more interpretive key in reading this parable: 12:46–50. In this conversation, preceding the telling of the parable, Jesus pointed to the disciples to be the new household. Within this new household, the disciples would do the will of the Father because the Father was the head of the household. His wish would be their command. What was his command? Based on the parable, most likely the Father's will had to do with sowing the word of the kingdom message. Contrary to the seemingly discouraging message of the parable itself, the whole story became an encouragement. This work regardless of results was the Father's will, simply because God was in charge (i.e., kingdom of heaven).

PUTTING THE TEXT IN HISTORY:
MEANINGS FOR THE WORLD OF AUTHOR-READERS

By the time Matthew wrote these words, Judea was not in as good a shape as before 70 CE. Many Jews had been displaced by the war with the Romans. They were in a second exile. The political chaos in the empire showed no hope for restoration of the national Israel. "God's people" would remain in their limbo. Although the Jews had a home they could call their own with their limited governance, 70 CE had robbed them of any hope. As a spiritual location, Judea had quickly turned into a drying oasis.

In light of the patron-client society of the first century, Matthew's audience would be in the minority. Not only were they Jews, they were also Jewish followers of Jesus. They were the minority among the minority. They were the outsiders among outsiders. Yet, Matthew's Jesus turned the table on the whole situation. In exact parallel with Jesus' story situation, Matthew's audience was much like the disciples, isolated with Jesus and doomed to a crucified failure. Hope against hope, however, this same group would be the remnant that would lead God's people to a harvest. Telling them the parable would be too weak of an encouragement, but prefacing it with the Isaiah 6 passage would pack a huge punch. Thus, the story of Isaiah 6 certainly fits perfectly with the patron-client situation with Jesus (and Matthew) being the patron of this new community. This small group would draw encouragement from such a story of Jesus to know its importance in God's salvation history.

In terms of corporate personality, Matthew's Jesus identified the disciples as his in-group. The sower in the story then became a type of all those who carried the word to unknown and unchartered territories. Such a group would encounter difficulty, not only as individuals but also as a group. The parable depicted some of their common encounters with the world. Every person, then, would not think that the difficulty was hers and hers alone. Rather, someone else somewhere within the Christ-following community would encounter the very same thing. The struggle would not only be against things outside of the religious community but also encountered within the community of Judaism (i.e., Israel could have been Jesus' soil). As the followers of Christ became alienated, they had to rely on stories like this one to get through the alienation as a group. Their identity was no longer primarily with their kin who rejected them. They had a new identity in Jesus, drawn from the Old Testament exile remnant.

For those in the Christian faith community, the parable here definitely speaks loudly about the place of this community in today's world. Matthew's Jesus never promised that things would go well for his followers. Instead, this parable negated an easy life. Most believers want to have the backward telling of the parable, planning for all the hope to be realized. Matthew's Jesus did not use the large crowd to accomplish his kingdom immediately either. We live in a world, driven by efficiency and statistics. Results must happen yesterday! And if they do not, we quickly try to improve things. The parable teaches that results do not always happen in the way the faith community expects them. In fact, the results almost seem random, at times, left up to chance. Chance seems to be all that was left when the sower randomly threw the seeds in the parable. Without Jesus' presupposition from the Isaiah 6 narrative, the Christian faith is a faith of pure chance. With Isaiah 6, however, it becomes a delayed but progressive hope.

There is yet one more aspect about this parable that strikes at the heart of modern Christian ministry paradigm. The sower seems quite random in his work. He did not prepare the soil and figure out his target audience. The way we often do "church" today is very driven by preparation work and methods. We host many seminars on the best methods and so on. The backward telling of this story shows a smooth growth in the kingdom because the method is right. Jesus went the opposite direction. In his story, the sower just spread the seed on whatever path he came across. While this was bad farming practice, Jesus deliberately used a bad practice to show that not every single work of the word would be neatly methodical. Not every work can find the perfect target audience. Not every method can prepare people to hear the word. The sower acted like he did not know. Today's faith is much more packaged with quite efficient targeting, packaging, and marketing schemes. I have even read an article recently that sees this parable as teaching to prepare the soil properly. Such a modern, Western, strategy-oriented reading discolors Jesus' parable.

Although the New Testament might have indicated elsewhere about mission strategy, this parable has nothing to say about the neatly strategic modern mission, but it does speak outside of that modern paradigm. With so many advances in strategy in mission, the spontaneous "sow as you go" mentality is absent in many modern Christian communities. Jesus' parable basically challenged Matthew's audience to choose to "sow as you go." The simple yet beautiful (even possibly whimsical) paradigm may be the shot in the arm modern spirituality needs. Perhaps more spontaneity of Jesus' kingdom paradigm is needed for the organized modern faith. Resistance against Roman colonial dominance was not the tact many used in the Jewish war. Rather, they spread kingdom seeds via the word, as the community moved from place to place.

What should the present faith community do based on this parable? The emphasis on the word certainly is clear. The faith community must not abandon a strong understanding of the kingdom message, not only of what it meant back in those days, but what it means now and how it plays out today. This effort should require both vigorous intellectual reflection and robust activism. Whether the community reaches all the desired results, standing still is not the option presented by this parable.

My readers will notice that in my backward telling of the parable, I first eliminated the Isaiah 6 quotation and then smoothed out the seemingly silly way of sowing into something that makes perfect sense in both Jesus' world and ours. After all, the strange world of Jesus' parable shows the sower doing something quite random and silly. His whimsical sowing deserves a reprimand from the farming expert in his day and ours. Everything was left up to chance. Why not move the obstacles? That is the precise point, isn't it? The obstacles were there with this unusual way of sowing. The entire effort of the kingdom message or the word seems quite out of the norm. The entire effort seems silly. Without Isaiah 6, the entire effort seems like a mindless and idiotic gamble. With Isaiah 6, Jesus' message, all of a sudden, gives hope.

God's way might seem completely different from human convention and utterly hopeless, but from that downright despairing moment came hope. Just like the final crop would yield a hundred, sixty, and thirty times the original seed, so does hope. Who is to say that such random sowing cannot yield surprisingly manifold results? Such is the force of Jesus' parable. Ministry can sometimes seem to be mindless and fruitless, much like the parable and Isaiah 6. An impossible mission is not necessarily a bad mission.

For preachers who want to create a faithful retelling of Jesus' story through Matthew, I have the follow suggested outline that reflects my work above.

Title: Mission Made Impossible?
Telling It Backwards: A well-prepared soil for seeding . . . but the kingdom is not like that! How would the kingdom work if the soil was not prepared?

1) The challenge of kingdom work (13:18–23)
2) The hope of kingdom work (13:11–17)
3) The exclusiveness of kingdom work (13:1–10)
Conclusion: You aren't alone, but you may never be the majority.
Sow as you go!

REFLECTION QUESTIONS

1. How does the elimination of the Isaiah 6 quotation impact the entire hearing of the parable?

2. What other ways of sowing were available in Jesus' day?

3. Why did Jesus choose this way of sowing to illustrate his point?

4. What did the telling of the story mean to Matthew's audience?

5. How would such a parable impact modern faith and practice?

2

Hunting for Weeds in the Midst of Wheat?

TELLING IT BACKWARD: MATTHEW 13:24-30

> He presented them with another parable: "The kingdom of heaven is like a person who sowed good seed in his field. But during the night, an enemy came and sowed weeds among the wheat and went away. When the plants sprouted and bore grain, then the weeds also appeared. So the slaves of the owner came and said to him, 'Sir, didn't you sow good seed in your field? Then where did the weeds come from?' The owner, having kept watch the last few months, said, 'An enemy has done this.' So the slaves replied, 'Do you want us to go and gather them?' The owner said, 'I've attempted to stop the enemy and have largely succeeded. What you have here is the leftover. Go ahead and sort out the bad plants. So what if you uproot a few good plants? It is well worth it.'"

I TELL JESUS' STORY backwards based on the normal sowing practices of Jesus' day (and today). In those days, it would take the seed a few months to grow. Its growth would not be visible so quickly, at least not overnight. Thus, I have normalized the story Jesus told to give it less of a fairy-tale feel. In a land of rivalry and competition for honor, landowners probably hired security to keep an eye on the farm. Most likely, the security force would have found the enemy eventually, if this went on for a few months. Logically, they would have taken care of the impure plants fairly quickly as the enemy could not have gone too far before being caught. If by chance bad seeds did get sown, most likely the servants would take out the weeds to prevent them from taking up the nutrition in the soil for the good plants. This is the reason why the servants asked the owner. This is why the owner above told the servants to clean out the weeds before they grew too big. The problem would therefore be solved immediately from every front. Yet, neither Jesus nor Matthew told the story in this backward fashion.

TELLING IT NORMAL: KEY ELEMENTS IN THE STORY

24 He presented them with another parable: "The kingdom of heaven is like a person who sowed good seed in his field. 25 But while everyone was sleeping, an enemy came and sowed weeds among the wheat and went away. 26 When the plants sprouted and bore grain, then the weeds also appeared. 27 So the slaves of the owner came and said to him, 'Sir, didn't you sow good seed in your field? Then where did the weeds come from?' 28 He said, 'An enemy has done this.' So the slaves replied, 'Do you want us to go and gather them?' 29 But he said, 'No, since in gathering the weeds you may uproot the wheat with them. 30 Let both grow together until the harvest. At harvest time I will tell the reapers, 'First collect the weeds and tie them in bundles to be burned, but then gather the wheat into my barn.'"

36 Then he left the crowds and went into the house. And his disciples came to him saying, "Explain to us the parable of the weeds in the field." 37 He answered, "The one who sowed the good seed is the Son of Man. 38 The field is the world and the good seed are the people of the kingdom. The weeds are the people of the evil one, 39 and the enemy who sows them is the devil. The harvest is the end of the age, and the reapers are angels. 40 As the weeds are collected and burned with fire, so it will be at the end of the age. 41 The Son of Man will send his angels, and they will gather from his kingdom everything that causes sin as well as all lawbreakers. 42 They will throw them into the fiery furnace, where there will be weeping and gnashing of teeth. 43 Then the righteous will shine like the sun in the kingdom of their Father. The one who has ears had better listen!

While Jesus talked about the singular seed and singular sower in the previous parable, he now talked about the result of sowing. This story is much like the previous one, in that Jesus gave an explanation in private in 13:36–43.

In fact, careful readers will notice that all that way up to 13:43, the parables are all related to seed. Evidently, the parallel of 13:9 and 13:43 shows these parables to be related. Most likely, the weed parable is a continuation of the previous sowing parable. It is highly unlikely that Jesus (or Matthew, in his arrangement) meant for them to be interpreted individually without keeping in context with one another. The plot goes something like this.

The location of the parable itself was in the field (13:24). The enemy who sowed some bad seeds overnight had caused the weed to grow among the wheat (13:26). Eventually, probably after a few months, the servants saw the weed coming up with the wheat (13:27). Surprisingly, the owner acted like he knew that the enemy sowed bad seeds (13:28a). Several possibilities existed for the confidence the owner showed about the enemy. Either he saw the enemy but did not stop him (which makes no sense) or he was completely confident that all his seeds were good. The second possibility is stronger. The owner had no doubt that the seed he had was good. The servants then wanted to ask whether they ought to pull out the bad plants (13:28b). Many identify the weed to be a wheat-like plant that carried a poisonous fungus that could be mistakenly grounded into wheat flour.[1] The owner said to delay the eradication of weeds until the harvesting of wheat, when the bad could be separated from the good without ever endangering the good (13:29–30).

The two seed parables (in 13:19–23 and 13:24–30) naturally draw comparison. The beginnings of both parables talk about the kingdom. There is no doubt about the integrity of the seed sown by the original sower. Both parables show varying results, with the first one showing three bad soils along with one good soil and the second one showing a mixture of results within the same soil. The first parable (i.e., 13:19–23) focuses on distinction of different kinds of recipients. The second parable here (i.e., 13:24–30) appears to be talking about a mixed result in the same field. The first parable seems to point to fully obvious results, while the second parable brings an element of surprise. It would look something like this.

Kingdom (13:19)	Kingdom (13:24)
Two results, four soils (13:20–23)	Two results, one soil (13:25–26)
	The owner's solution (13:27–30)

1. Snodgrass, *Stories with Intent*, 198.

Thus, the parables start out similarly but end up with a noteworthy difference. The difference, base on the above simple plot chart shows the owner's solution in 13:27–30. I am not suggesting that somehow Jesus (or Matthew, more likely) had laid out in his mind some plot diagram above before telling the stories. I am however suggesting that Jesus had followed some kind of rough formula much like the cliché "Once upon a time . . ." of his day that looks like the above layout in his oral delivery of the parable. All he did was add to the sower parable to create a new story. The oral modification really was not all that hard, much like the inexact improvisation of modern jazz. Based on the above layout, the real key to understanding is the owner's suggestion. We must pay attention to this outstanding aspect from the form of the parable.

What is the meaning of the parable? If we observe the parable itself, it seems to indicate that Jesus was telling something like a fable. Jesus' parable did not focus on the lengthy process for a seed to become visibly harmful in plant form. It would take a little while before its growth became visible, and someone finally noticed the mature plant. Maybe Jesus was saying that evil was always lurking underneath a good community. Jesus seemed to focus a little more on how long it took for evil to show its face. Based on this plot, Jesus gave a very simple explanation.

As Jesus continued his explanation, this parable turns into an allegory. This time, Jesus was clear about the sower being the Son of Man (13:37), the field being the world (13:38), the seed being the sons of the kingdom (13:38), and the enemy being the devil (13:39). Straight away, the reader will notice that this parable functions quite differently than the previous sower parable, though there is continuity with that parable. While the previous sower parable points to the disciples' (or any messenger of the kingdom's) future, this parable points to the end of the age. While the previous parable talks of bearing fruit, the harvest was not referring to humans. In light of what is prior to the previous parable in 12:50, and the seed being the kingdom message or the word, the harvest was probably a general description of any outcome that matches kingdom characteristics.

Here, the seed is a collective singular of the faith community, those who belonged to the kingdom. The singular seed in 13:37 demonstrates a typological function of the seed. In fact, Matthew used the collective single to describe the seed throughout this parable.[2] In some ways, this collective

---

2. The "son of" designation is an Aramaic expression for having a character of somebody or some idea. Here, they have the character of kingdom citizens.

description is Jesus' way of saying to the disciples, "This seed represents all of you together showing kingdom characteristics of a good plant." However, in this world, all was not well. There would be other kinds of communities (i.e., plants from the devil's seed). These communities, like seed, would not be immediately noticeable until they started bearing weeds. Evil was not obvious at the onset. While Jesus explained many elements of the parable, yet Jesus did not explain a few characters, either because they were readily obvious to the audience or because they were not really important. The owner of the field had no identity. Neither did the servants. There is no reason to suggest that this conversation between the owner and the servants is unimportant, according to the plot diagram in the above discussion. These characters did have an ethical conversation. What would the servants' function be?

It is probably more important to discuss their ethical function rather than identifying them definitively and symbolically. The conversation between the owner and the servants did not receive any explanation probably because its moral was readily obvious. Within the kingdom community, there were probably some who would want to root out the weeds. Probably the disciples would identify themselves with the servants. This conversation shows that the solution was not to root them out immediately but to wait until God rooted them and their children out at the end by his harvesting angels (13:40–41). These children caused the sin and evil that did not belong to the kingdom. Jesus and his angels would root both the existence and cause of evil out at the end. In other words, the function of the conversation was to teach an ethic of delay. This delayed ethic fits perfectly God's delayed judgment within the plot of the parable. By now, we must figure out that even when God was in charge (i.e., kingdom of heaven), bad seeds could still be sowed to create chaos among the wheat.

The setting of this parable is important for understanding it fully. We must notice the form of the entire story from 13:1–43 because this story shares the same characteristic of private explanation. Therefore, the modern interpreter ought to make 13:10–17 part of the guiding interpretive principle to shed light not only on Jesus' words, but also his actions. There is no need to explain 13:10–17 here, as the previous chapter has already given adequate discussion. What would it mean, though, in light of Jesus' explanation of this parable?

This private teaching of Jesus, much like the previous private teaching, was only relevant for Jesus' followers—not for the crowd. The Isaiah 6 exile story would eventually talk about a remnant at the end of the book. This remnant would come out of the exile. Here however the picture was far from ideal. Instead of having a pure group coming out of the exile, the devil had sown different kinds of evil people to oppose the cause. This had indeed happened in the return from exile. This pattern would happen again at Jesus' kingdom. This parable taught important ethics in light of delayed judgment. The children of the kingdom could fight these evildoers with all their energy, but Jesus urged them not to waste energy on what God would do later at the end of time (i.e., the final judgment). Instead, this parable complements the previous parable in urging the disciples to focus more on bearing a good harvest of kingdom work. By including the final judgment, this parable has created an eschatological ethic. What would Jesus have them do to bear a harvest? Based on the previous parable, they were to spread the seed of the word.

PUTTING THE TEXT IN HISTORY: MEANINGS FOR THE WORLD OF AUTHOR-READERS

Jesus' simple parable and explanation have huge implications for Matthew's audience. Matthew's audience faced enormous pressure in this chaotic time. With the Roman defeat of the Jewish rebels, Matthew's audience had been unsettled with little hope on the horizon. Under colonial rule, the prospect of recreating the revolutionary force was slim. Being followers of a crucified criminal would not have helped their cause, given the fact that crucifixion was often the punishment for non-citizen revolutionaries. They faced a grimmer reality than those who chose not to consider Jesus as lord and messiah. There were many kinds of evil around, from possible greater persecution to an ostracized existence. They probably had questions as to whether God was in charge (i.e., kingdom of heaven) of the growth of the faith community. The problem of theodicy was never greater for these followers of Jesus. There is really no solution, even though they probably had an apocalyptic expectation of the imminent second advent of the Son of Man.

In the society (i.e., the world in the parable), people benefited from having the proper relational connections. This would put Matthew's audience at a huge disadvantage because of the evil prevalent in this society. Their new identity as kingdom citizens would automatically exclude them from many advantageous situations. It would be easier for them to use power to sort out the evildoers and exert their new belief. Matthew's Jesus discouraged them from using the world's system to gain for the kingdom. Since their reward would be in the future, their present course should not be focused on pulling weed or on commiseration. This story assured them that there would be a greater future when they, the oppressed, would receive their just reward at the final divine judgment—if they stayed the course.

This parable has many possible pitfalls for misapplication in today's world. It can give the false message that Jesus does not need his followers today to fight evil and right the wrongs of the world. Yet, Jesus continued to have very harsh things to say about his own faith community. Many of his apostles continued to address the shortfalls of their own faith community. In light of the first-century social situation, Matthew's Jesus probably was not prohibiting the fight against injustice, per se. If the seed was in the world, there is no possible way to eradicate all the evil from the world. Matthew's Jesus named the evil, without necessarily going on a witch-hunt for weeds, but encouraged the followers to do what they could to demonstrate kingdom righteousness. Witch-hunting would not be the tact for the kingdom. God would be the final judge against the evil that humans would be unable to uproot. The kingdom citizen ought to trust in that promise of future judgment. If this parable analogizes the kingdom, then the kingdom goes against our self-righteous instincts when we first perceive evil.

In the Christian world right now, especially among evangelicals, witch-hunting has turned into a full-time job for some preachers, theologians, coalitions, and bloggers. Their battle wages heatedly on two fronts: both inside and outside of the church. Within the church, people often use the Bible to (in the words of one blogger) "enforce boundaries."[3] Or better yet, we use our interpretation of the Bible to enforce boundaries often without rational and gracious dialogue. Some have written book-length polemics against those with different interpretations on debatable aspects of the faith. The goal, advertently or otherwise, is to send out religious watchdogs to sniff out the heretics. Even asking one sensitive question could get one bitten, let alone providing alternate answers. Along with the penchant to find the most "unorthodox" among believers, unreasonable name-calling ensues. Such argument would spill out in the church's posture to the outside. Hot-button issues that the church considers to be top priority naturally result in polemics that neither give the church a voice nor a

---

3. http://www.patheos.com/blogs/slacktivist/2013/02/06/white-evangelical
-gatekeeping-a-particularly-ugly-example-in-real-time/

place in society. More importantly, the owner's words in 13:29 point out the possibility of innocent victims being sacrificed on the altar of what the witch-hunter considers the truth. The drama some modern evangelicals create resembles the backward tale I first told at the beginning of this chapter, rather than the way Matthew's Jesus told this parable, and violates the most important ethical conversation between the owner and the servants. Such obsession with hunting down the bad guy works directly against the way Jesus envisioned his kingdom.

What was the ethical response to all the weeds? Matthew's Jesus described the elect as being the "righteous" in 13:43. It is important not to read the Reformed idea of imputed righteousness or justification by faith here. The best definition of righteousness in Matthew comes out of 6:1–18 where righteousness is clearly measured by deeds with the right motive, to be seen by God and not merely by humans. The best expression of God being in charge (i.e., kingdom of heaven) is community righteousness that honors God. Thus, righteousness is a balance of proper deeds and motives including, but not limited to, almsgiving to the poor, prayer, and fasting (6:1–18). The measurement of this righteousness comes from God. Thus, those who are in the kingdom of God ought to perform righteous deeds as an act of worship towards the real king, God himself. The acts of righteousness exclude witch-hunting. It also excludes self-righteousness. Faith can come out of kingdom righteousness that believes in the final divine judgment. By telling the parable, Matthew was basically saying, "You must choose between obsessing about where the weeds are, or moving in the righteous direction. Righteousness is best."

There are certain risks when preaching this text as is, because Matthew's concern might not be ours. Matthew's own definition of evil might not be the same as ours. For example, it is hard to apply strictly what it says if we just let go of all the evildoers. What about child molesters in the church? Certainly, that sort of action would be viewed with great disdain in Matthew's community. What about charlatans who defraud offerings from congregations? Again, the parable's view of wealth (e.g., 13:22) would negate letting those who abuse power and money get away easily. The parable was not some kind of excuse for absolute neglect to do justice in the church. Certainly, the church should be a place of justice. The parable seems to emphasize the primary focus of the kingdom and the certainty of the eschatological judgment. The focus was obviously not trying to hunt down every witch. When the church focuses on the witch-hunt, the faith gets derailed from the kingdom track. The following is the suggested sermon outline based on all the above work that has been done on this passage.

Title: Good Seeds in a World with Evil
Telling It Backward: Uprooting a few good ones to save the rest . . . but the kingdom value is not like that. What do we do with hidden evil in our midst?

1) Sowing Two Kinds of Seeds (13:24–28, 36–39a)
2) Two Kinds of Endings (13:29–30, 39b–43)
3) Tasks for the Seeds Now (13:27–28): acts of righteousness with the right motive
Conclusion: Instead of pointing out every evil, the faith community must do its best to do every good as it awaits the final judgment.

REFLECTION QUESTIONS

1. What part of the parable is the key ethical point and why?

2. What was the purpose of the parable?

3. How did the parable address Matthew's situation?

4. How does the parable speak to the modern church?

5. What danger does the backward tale contain?

3

The Large Challenge of Being Small

TELLING IT BACKWARD: MATTHEW 13:31-35

> He gave them another parable: "The kingdom of heaven is like a mustard seed. It is the smallest of all the seeds. Wind and animals carry the seeds all over the place. No deliberate sowing is necessary to yield any reasonable harvest, though a man grabbed a bunch of such seeds and sowed them to create his own harvest. As the smallest seed however, when it has grown it is the greatest garden plant and becomes a tree, so that the wild birds come and nest in its branches."

> He told them another parable: "The kingdom of heaven is like yeast that a woman took and mixed with any measure of flour until all the dough had risen."

IN THE US, "BIGGER is better" commercials are a dime a dozen. One particularly striking commercial has a host asking a bunch of little kids whether bigger or smaller is better. The conclusion is that bigger is better—and the phone company in the commercial has the largest 4G system, which makes it better. This American obsession with size only becomes clearer to me after living overseas in England and in Hong Kong. Certainly, our country often has the best deal the almighty dollar can buy. For instance, our restaurant meals have huge portions. Jesus' parable is anything but this "big" American dream.

I have chosen to put the two parables together both for convenience and for their placement within Matthew 13. As we have already stated above, two major seed parables in 13:1–30 and 13:36–34 have enclosed the unit neatly with Jesus' private ministry. Enclosed within are these two very short parables. It is then reasonable to view them together for their brevity and placement. Soon enough, we shall see their similarity.

The backward telling of this story shows how strange it is for a man to plant "one" seed. The mustard seed is slightly bigger than a dandelion seed. No one plants dandelion seeds. Dandelions grow naturally, being spread by the wind. To sow one seed does not accord well with reality. No one grabs one tiny seed to plant it. Rather, better version would have the seeds fly all over the place so much so that the mustard plant overgrows and takes over the entire field.

The flour and yeast story really does not need to be told backward, but we can take the measurement element out. After all, the function of the yeast is to cause flour to rise. Whether the dough is large or small, the yeast will cause a rise. Why indeed do we need a measurement? The above stories can easily represent reality if the sower did not only sow one seed, but Jesus also gave no prescribed measurement of the dough in the yeast parable. Yet, neither Jesus nor Matthew told the story in the fashion above.

TELLING IT NORMAL: KEY ELEMENTS IN THE STORY

> 31 He gave them another parable: "The kingdom of heaven is like a mustard seed that a man took and sowed in his field. 32 It is the smallest of all the seeds, but when it has grown it is the greatest garden plant and becomes a tree, so that the wild birds come and nest in its branches."

> 33 He told them another parable: "The kingdom of heaven is like yeast that a woman took and mixed with three measures of flour until all the dough had risen."

Jesus' parables here are really a Facebook story. They address our modern worldview directly. We shall see later how this story is like the Facebook story.

These two parables are essentially similar because they both deal with "smallness." The amount taken out of the modified version of the parables is the key. The plot of the mustard seed parable starts with the man sowing a singular mustard seed. This indicates the need for the mustard plant. Then, the plant grew into a "tree." Then, the tree served to house birds as a nesting place. Several spectacular parts of this story should catch the attention of the listener.

First, the fact a sower planted one mustard seed is unusual, to say the least. This planting of a single seed shows the smallness of the seed but at the same time shows intention of the sower. It was not sown at random. It was sown deliberately and unusually in this manner. Probably the reason was to show the smallness of one seed that would grow into a "tree." Second, the fact Jesus called the plant a tree is unusual. Mustard plants are not strictly trees. Yet some of them could grow well over the human height, tall enough to nest birds underneath it. Third, the fact Jesus used a common saying about nesting birds should also draw attention because the same analogy was used of the kingdom in Ezekiel 17:22–24. Although the plant in Ezekiel was not a mustard plant, Jesus used a familiar story to illustrate God's plan in restoring his people, just like the time of Ezekiel.

I am unsure whether Jesus literally had Ezekiel 17 in mind or whether he was using a popular metaphor that dated back to Ezekiel's day for birds' nesting habits. It is also dangerous to read into the bird's behavior all kinds of malevolent implications of demonic forces. These are birds! The fact that the mustard plant provided enough coverage for the birds to nest shows that the mustard plant had become much greater than its original seed form. In summary, Jesus simply wanted to express the greatness of the small seed. This greatness was deliberately and not accidentally sown to show how something seemingly insignificant could grow into something so great. In the next story, Jesus switched emphasis.

The second story goes something like this. The baker got some yeast of uncertain amount, presumably not a lot, and then worked the yeast into a huge piece of dough close to fifty pounds. Such a huge piece could feed an entire banquet. Fifty pounds of dough, around three measures of flour, would be a huge amount. The gigantic dough shows that the baker had to knead the dough through hard work to help it rise. Jesus told of the huge amount to show the largeness of the impact the little yeast had. With that smallness however came hard work. This element of hard work did not exist in the previous parable about the mustard seed. The small amount is definitely important in the same way as the mustard seed. Like the mustard plant serving the purpose of housing the birds, the bread that came out of the dough could feed a lot of people.

From both stories, Jesus gave the exact amount of the seed and the dough. The difference is that the mustard seed parable focused on the smallness of the seed, and that the yeast parable focused on the largeness of the dough. Thus, Jesus both appreciated the smallness of the beginning, the largeness of the challenge, the arduousness of the labor, and ultimately the surprising result. During the time when Jesus first spoke these parables, his movement was tiny in comparison to other movements in the Jewish world. Jesus' movement was so small that he did not receive much attention even in the Jewish historian Josephus's writing. The narrator then explained why he told the parables in 13:34–35. Matthew drew from Psalm 78:2 in 13:35 to explain why Jesus told all the parables, not just these two stories. Jesus had told stories to the crowd generally but explained the meanings to the disciples specifically. Since the creation of the world, these ideas were not obvious, according to Matthew. The idea of sowing to create a kingdom harvest, the idea of the existence of evildoers, and the greatness of the kingdom impact were all veiled until this point. Jesus' work was to unveil these ideas. Matthew probably used Psalm 78 for good reason.

During synagogue worship, people regularly sang entire Psalms and did not quote them at random. Psalm 78 is a fantastic Psalm proclaiming God's wise dealings with Israel (Ps 78:2–4). Psalm 78 gives continuity to Israel's present with Israel's past. The present Israel would have to learn from historical mistakes of the past (Ps 78:8). If we read within the larger context of Psalm 78, the parables of Jesus make sense. Jesus' parables ended on a high note. God's work, though quite small like the mustard seed or yeast, ended up impacting the world in miraculous proportion. This work was not an accident, as the mustard seed parable shows. Like the singular mustard seed being deliberately sowed, any impact was no accident but was under the direct control of the sower. Perhaps, Matthew's message is much broader than Jesus'. By citing Psalm 78, Matthew was saying that God's work in the past was indeed great, but the greatest work was yet veiled until Jesus came with these parables. Jesus' work would be God's greatest work. While the kingdom work was visible in the past, the present work by Jesus would become its fullest expression. In Matthew 13, the story started with sowing of the seed that seems random with post-exile narrative but ended with the promise of great results. God's work was never going to be obvious. Neither was it predictable. Jesus' teaching however gave certainty of hope. The disciples were first to receive this message because they would be at the center of this great work.

This great work is a mini-climax in Matthew's writing, especially when we read it in light of the greater context. Starting in Matthew 10, Jesus sent out the twelve and they were not going to have an easy time (10:32–39). The question would confront readers, "If God was at work, shouldn't the work be easy?" The hard time continued in Matthew 11 where even John the Baptist was asking Jesus whether he was the one to come for God's mission. Without a little irony, John himself who did God's work had to send people to ask Jesus because he himself was sitting in prison, presumably waiting for his own death. The movement was on the verge of complete and irrecoverable shipwreck. As if John's imprisonment was not horrible enough, cities would outright refuse Jesus' message while religious authorities continued to reject Jesus' form of Judaism (11:20—12:37). Even with Jesus' many great works, the religious authorities refused to see any legitimacy in his work (12:38–45). This new faith was one generation from extinction. Jesus told these parables in Matthew in such a gloomy context. The parables became the Big Bang in the midst of Israel's darkness. Just because the faith community was small and the challenge was gigantic, God had never lost his sovereign charge. Yet, even with the promise of growth, Jesus forced his audience to choose hard work.

PUTTING THE TEXT IN HISTORY: MEANINGS FOR THE WORLD OF AUTHOR-READERS

It is absolutely easy to read these parables as if they were realized in Matthew's day. Matthew's situation was not much different from Jesus'. Christianity was not an official religion, with relatively small number of believers. Within the vast Empire, it hardly made a drop of impact. As a small movement, its followers had to rely on its integration into that society in order to survive. One way Matthew's audience would integrate was to allow non-Jewish believers into their community (28:18–20) in their quest of making disciples of all nations, not just Jews. All the while, they would keep their minority status both in faith and in number. Would a minority be able to make any impact at all? The greatest expression of God's charge (i.e., kingdom of heaven) was having small community making an eventually great impact. Matthew's Jesus was presenting a hopeful future, while showing that great impact was possible.

When dealing with relationships, Matthew's audience would face the issue of how they would identify with the groups around him. In their mission, relational transactions that were formerly beneficial to them, especially with the synagogue, would no longer help them. In some ways, their new alliance with some gentile converts would create a new hybrid and assimilation into the Empire. However they had to face a realistic problem; these gentile groups had used imperialism to ruin their worship experience in the temple, and might have, in some cases, killed their family members. Loving enemies and ministering to them was not going to be easy. It was hard work just like the large piece of dough.

When reading this story as an Asian, I am reminded by a speech by Michael Oh, the new CEO of the Lausanne Movement. Oh talked movingly about being a Korean-American who was raised on the narrative of Japanese slaughter and rape in World War II. He then talked about the Lord's call for him to be a missionary academic in Japan, the very country that inflicted such pain to his kin. Oh's ministry in Lausanne would have to include ethnic Japanese. This mission would bring reconciliation and forgiveness, but none of it would come easy. Many diaspora Asians in America also had similar experiences. Ethnic Chinese and Japanese are no longer enemies when they both believe in the way of Jesus, and have created Asian-American churches that included former enemy groups as part of the greater expression of Jesus' kingdom.

The struggle of identity would continue for Matthew's audience, but this struggle would lessen, as the greater impact of disciple making of gentiles became a reality. Their ethnic distinction would not fade but would allow for inclusion of gentiles without making gentiles exactly like them. The community of Jesus would allow both to exist under the same roof, making an unusual impact.

When thinking about today's faith, Matthew's message addresses the faith community differently. Christianity has become one of the great religions of the ancient world, but at the same time, there is some real angst about western society being post-Christian. Believers are so fearful that many have made their enemy the secular society. Their fear, though sometimes reasonable, is still largely misguided. Jesus' way was never about fighting the Romans. Neither was Jesus' way about being the dominant religion. Numerical dominance had already been negated in the four soils with only one soil having the ability to bear a harvest in 13:18–23. Matthew's Jesus is at least consistent about numbers. In fact, the greatest impact the faith had was when it was weak, much like the seed or the yeast. Unlike our expectation of things becoming easier, Jesus never dismissed hard work.

Many today are living my backward story rather than Jesus' story. They somehow expect no hard work and numerical advantage from the growth of Christianity. Some have stopped being a visible witness out in society by doing good work among those who need it. Some churches focus on growing numerically and limit their ministry to within the four walls (and "programs") of the church. Number, even being a minority, should never be a worry for the faith community. At the same time, its weakest state can also show its supernatural power the most but not without deliberate hard work. Strength does not come from numerical advantage but from hard work through faith, much like the baker who kneaded the yeast into the gigantic piece of dough. Faith that came out of hope was strongest when all situations looked grim in Matthew's time. The same must be true today. If there were a hopeful sermon for today, these parables would be it because they put faith and work in their proper place for kingdom impact.

If we were to preach a sermon based on these wonderful texts, Jesus' stories are about impact of impossibly small things. I am a big Facebook user. Most of my readers can find me on Facebook to chat about my writing ideas and their own thoughts.[1] Facebook was a free social network founded in 2004 in a university dorm room. Its founding was more like an accident of genius, than an intentional business plan. Originally, Mark Zuckerberg, a brilliant Harvard student, and a few of his friends created a website to vote on the attractiveness of fellow students. The university shut them down. Zuckerberg and his friends then founded a social network group only for Harvard. The success of this work eventually expanded to other elite universities. Today, this whimsical and fun beginning has resulted in more users than the population of some countries in the world. Facebook has become a nation unto itself. The difference of course with Jesus' parable is that the smallness was more than a whimsical fun. God planned it in the kingdom of heaven, and the ending, according to Matthew's Jesus, is going to be so much greater than any human invention. In an age of instant satisfaction, the yeast parable also encourages modern readers to see the impossibly small yeast needing hard work in the gigantic challenge presented by the dough. Kneading takes time, patience, and hard work. For the greatest impact, time, patience, and hard work are indispensible. Knowing God is in charge (i.e., kingdom of heaven) ought to drive the community to work

---

1. My readers usually can reach me here on Facebook to share their ideas. https://www.facebook.com/drsamtsang.

harder against the great challenge. For preachers who want to attempt to teach and preach these parables, the following structure might help.

Title: When kingdom work seems small . . .
Telling It Backward: The seeds are randomly and have little impact . . . but the kingdom does not work like that. There is so much good news these days. How can there be good news?

1) The power of a singular seed (13:31–35)
2) The enormous work on the block of dough (13:36–33)
Conclusion: Size is overrated. Dynamite comes in small packages because of God's plan. Hard work is the key. Good news will come.

REFLECTION QUESTIONS

1. How does the singular seed point the way of interpretation?

2. What does the weight of the dough have to do with the meaning of the yeast parable?

3. What kind of message does Ps 78:2 add to this series of parables by Jesus?

4. What challenges did Matthew's audience have to face?

5. How do Jesus' parables here address the increasingly secularized western society?

4

Finding and Keeping

TELLING IT BACKWARD: MATTHEW 13:44-46

> Jesus told this parable: "The kingdom of heaven is like a treasure, hidden in a field, that a person found and sold the treasure for a very large piece of land because the piece of land would be valuable where landowners held power over society."

"FINDERS KEEPERS" IS A concept that dates back to ancient Roman times. When people dive for shipwrecks in open water or hunt for treasure in abandoned land, they might run across material that originally belonged to somebody else. Under the "finders keepers" concept, the finder becomes the new owner. Many still live by that adage today as they run across wallets or cash.

My warped retelling of Jesus' story in 13:44 is what I call a "finders keepers" story. Someone accidentally ran across treasure in a field. No one knew. He could keep the treasure, sell it, and then use the money to invest in a large piece of land that would generate income for generations to come. No one would know. I have also taken out 13:45-46 temporarily. Even though 13:45-46 is a different parable, it seems to read perfectly as an additional (complementary?) explanation to the present story. The beauty of skipping over 13:45-46 is the ambiguity of 13:44. Yet, neither Jesus nor Matthew told the story in this backward fashion or skipped 13:45-46.

TELLING IT NORMAL: KEY ELEMENTS IN THE STORY

> 44 "The kingdom of heaven is like a treasure, hidden in a field, that a person found and hid. Then because of joy he went and sold all that he had and bought that field.
>
> 45 "Again, the kingdom of heaven is like a merchant searching for fine pearls. 46 When he found a pearl of great value, he went out and sold everything he had and bought it."

If the previous parables in 13:31–33 were about small things making big impact, this parable talks about how valuable relatively small treasure is in relation to the field in which it was buried. This very short story in 13:44 has many angles. When people find a treasure, they naturally keep it. Yet, in a rural setting like Jesus', people might grow suspicious of the newly rich because no middle class had yet emerged. Although they may be suspicious, they could not pin the problem definitively on the newly rich. For the owner of the treasure could sell the treasure and split part of the earning with the buyer to cover up the new wealth, slowly using the money to acquire other kinds of commodities. The buyer had many options, not just one, and certainly not the one stated by Jesus here. Jesus in this parable compared the kingdom to the whole event and not just a treasure hunt. Thus, in order to interpret what the kingdom was like, the entire story needs attention.

The beauty of this story is in its ambiguity. The finder here obviously kept the secret to himself. Even when the treasure was buried again, the owner of the land did not know this secret. The finder then gathered enough wealth to buy the land *and* the treasure. In other words, the gain was not merely the large amount in the treasure, but also the field that contained it. His investment would surpass his gain if he were just to keep the treasure to himself. In what way was this like the kingdom of heaven?

The finder gained enormously by going about the legal route, not just getting a quick gain by the treasure but also by the very useful land. In order to do this, the person had to sell all that he had. Apparently, he had enough to buy this plot, perhaps a small plot, of land. The kingdom of heaven would be an enormous gain that would go beyond the rare treasure. The joy this person experienced was based on the knowledge that great gain was available when he applied his secret knowledge. Perhaps, Jesus was saying that applying the knowledge would result in great gain. Instead of looking for instant gratification (i.e., keeping the treasure without buying a field), the person applied his knowledge for a longer term and greater gain. Quickness is not always wise. It also does not create maximum benefits. Growth of the kingdom, then, takes time and long-term investment. When God was in charge (i.e., kingdom of heaven), people would invest for the long haul.

If we just pause and look at the backward telling of the story, we can see that preciousness is also an aspect of the story. Many would limit their interpretation of this parable to be about preciousness. But if the finder had simply put the treasure away and found great joy, that in itself would have expressed the concept of preciousness. The way Jesus told it involved not just preciousness, but also a delayed strategy of gaining everything, from the treasure to the field. Thus, the whole kingdom of heaven parable here goes beyond the preciousness of the kingdom. Preciousness is presupposed, but patience is the focal point. Great profit from a precious discovery takes patience. The audience should choose patience over quick fixes. After all, Jesus would soon die and everything would seem lost. The kingdom requires patience.

Now, the telling of the treasure and field story works much better after it is linked with 13:45–46. While the previous parable presupposes preciousness but advocates other virtues, 13:45–46 tells the treasure and field story in the opposite direction. While 13:44 seems to recount an accidental discovery, the story in 13:45–46 does not. The merchant in 13:45–46 looked for a specific pearl. Merchants in Jesus' day would be familiar with the value of pearls, since they were often the mediating party in the trade of exotic and expensive goods. Instead of mediating one more deal among many exchanges of pearls, this merchant found one pearl he wanted for himself. A merchant was a man with experience in Jesus' day. He was unlike the laborer who ran into the hidden treasure. He had been eying different pearls throughout his life. He had looked at many options. He finally found the best option. This option was so precious that he gave up everything to gain it. By mentioning the main character as a merchant, Jesus was teaching about educated options. The merchant made a conscious choice after being educated in the options involving pearls.

The unavoidable interpretive strategy of reading the stories of the merchant with the treasure in the field shows all sides of the kingdom. Matthew's Jesus presupposed preciousness as the foundation for both stories. The merchant story is a progression from the treasure story. The treasure story has a sense of hiddenness about the treasure that the finder had to ponder over. The finder could see that the treasure was valuable, but the discovery was pure luck. The merchant story, though, shows another side to this whole kingdom parable. The merchant knew how much each pearl was worth, and finally found the best option after many educated examinations. Thus, Jesus used the treasure parable to teach on the patience and circumspection of the process of gaining *one* treasure. Jesus used the merchant parable to teach circumspection of looking at *many* possible pearls with *one* best choice. Jesus then was a realist who knew that many options were available. The reader could well fault the finder in the treasure story for an impulsive and amateurish move, but no one could fault the merchant for not knowing the many possible options. Besides Jesus' options, many good options were available in his day. Only the experienced and educated would choose the best option. All require patience.

The parables follow 13:36–43. This order is fascinating because it further explains why immediate weeding out of the field with two kinds of seeds is a bad idea because the kingdom is too precious (like a treasure) and contains too much (like the field with the pearls) to react too hastily, without thinking through the best options.

PUTTING THE TEXT IN HISTORY:
MEANINGS FOR THE WORLD OF AUTHOR-READERS

Based on the time of Matthew, there were many teachers and many options. Jesus was not teaching the only available way. There had been no shortage of options, from the time of the Jewish exile all the way to the destruction of the temple in 70 CE. Different options had different praxes that fit into the Roman society in different ways. With the destruction of the temple, some options, especially Zionist aspirations (with the exception of the later Bar-Kokhba), were eliminated.

Every option associated with Judaism or the likes of Judeo-Christian belief (an anachronistic label) had its own set of rules that defined the identity of each member. A practical concern also impacted the community. With the 70-CE temple destruction, many wondered whether the end of the age was near. People would be scrambling for options out of desperation. In mild panic and grave uncertainty, the Jewish believers whom Matthew addressed would be tempted to make a quick choice. The parables addressed such angsts. They assured the believers that God was in charge through his kingdom of heaven, but not everything would go according the desire of every believer.

The theme of preciousness in these parables points to the main reason why Jesus' option was best. The treasure and the pearl had lasting value back in Matthew's day. Jesus' kingdom was not only worth considering; it was worth serious study and reflection. Many scholars rightly note Matthew's focus on the teaching ministry of Jesus. Counter to the human knee-jerk instinct in such a situation, Matthew encouraged his audience not only to hold onto Jesus' teaching, but also to think deeply about it. With the confusion that surrounded Matthew's time, holding on that which was good, namely the teachings of Jesus, and gaining true knowledge of it would edify the discouraged. Such serious and deep reflection would ensure a great return on the investment into a good field and an expensive pearl.

My backward story once again exposes the way many modern believers live their faith. They focus on immediate gratification, even if they believe in the preciousness of the gospel. Consequently, they live in the backward narrative from Jesus' story. Some focus on the prosperity offered by a false gospel. Others use questionable means to simplify the gospel in order to get conversion results quickly. The parable demands a choice for patience and reflection, the very opposite of the quick fix of modern church evangelism. Those who rush headlong into the task simply miss the choice the parable demands of the readers.

Having resettled in the Seattle area, finding a residence remains quite the challenge I did not anticipate. Apparently, many cash-rich out-of-state immigrants have come to the area, causing home prices to rise. The rumor of a slow market remains a rumor. The Seattle housing market is hopping. One house stuck out among many. It was a run-down house over a huge lot. Even though the building material of this house is solid, its pretty stone fountain has toppled over. The adjacent empty lot that partly provides access to the house belongs to somebody else. This poor house had been sitting on the market for a long time. This house has a long outside corridor that links its different parts. If we examine it closely, this very large property, with huge square footages, is an estate. It is no mere run-down house. However, no one wanted to buy it because of its apparently run-down condition—until one educated buyer finally bought this underpriced property. If someone would repair it properly, the house would be worth almost twice the amount immediately. If . . . ! Many buyers possess a lot of cash, but not many have the insight to see the potential this run-down house possesses. It may take the new owner some time to save enough to buy the adjacent lot, but once he buys it, his earning potential will be substantially better than a finished house. Jesus' parables resemble such investment stories.

In today's world, with the internet, we want options. Matthew's Jesus did not try to hard sell the kingdom. At the same time, Matthew's Jesus was also not saying that all options are best. He suggested to us that options must be examined for what is good versus what is best. This is where we run into trouble. In today's electronic world, we are bombarded with so many options that we do not have the necessary time to give any in-depth examination to each one. As a result, the many Christian voices we hear become a vast ocean of superficiality.

If we were to preach a sermon from this discussion, the outline of the text may look something like this.

Title: Finding the Best Option
Telling It Backward: Whoever finds the treasure of the kingdom must quickly acquire it for himself . . . but the kingdom is not like that. What is the best tact in dealing with treasure?

1) Finders Keepers? (13:44)
2) Seekers Finders (13:45–46)
Conclusion: Good investment deserves deep reflection. Jesus' kingdom is the best possible deal, but it takes patience and reflection.

REFLECTION QUESTIONS

1. How does skipping 13:45–46 hurt the reading of 13:44?

2. What are the differences between the two related parables?

3. What are some of the reasons why the first parable does not turn into a "finders keepers" story?

4. What is the significance of the merchant's role in 13:45–46?

5. What modern stories can you think of that have a similar plot line as Jesus' two parables?

5

Fishing for the "Christian" Scribe

TELLING IT BACKWARD: MATTHEW 13:47-52

> Jesus told them this parable: "Again, the kingdom of heaven is like a net that was cast into the sea that caught all kinds of fish. When it was full, they pulled it ashore, sat down, gathered all the fish and sold them to both Jews and gentiles at the fish market. It will be this way at the end of the age.
>
> "Have you understood all these things?" They replied, "Yes." Then he said to them, "Therefore every expert in the law who has been trained for the kingdom of heaven is like the owner of a house who brings out of his treasure what is new and old."

I AM NOT A fisherman, but I have friends who are. Many fish for sporting purposes. Others do so for both sport and food. Most people who fish for food find ways to utilize nearly every fish. Even parts of the fish people do not use can be ground into chum, a form of bait. In other words, fishermen can use unused and uneaten fish for bait. Throwing away fish, unless for sporting purpose or preservation purpose, is not usually done by frugal fishermen. Imagine if I fish for a living. Every fish is worth something. Maybe one or two are no good, but I would not spend all day picking out the bad ones. The above story is based on how normal commercial fishermen would deal with the catch. Yet, neither Jesus nor Matthew told the story in this backward fashion. Neither Jesus nor Matthew was "normal."

TELLING IT NORMAL: KEY ELEMENTS IN THE STORY

> 47 "Again, the kingdom of heaven is like a net that was cast into the sea that caught all kinds of fish. 48 When it was full, they pulled it ashore, sat down, and put the good fish into containers and threw the bad away. 49 It will be this way at the end of the age. Angels will come and separate the evil from the righteous 50 and throw them into the fiery furnace, where there will be weeping and gnashing of teeth.

> 51 "Have you understood all these things?" They replied, "Yes." 52 Then he said to them, "Therefore every expert in the law who has been trained for the kingdom of heaven is like the owner of a house who brings out of his treasure what is new and old."

We have finally reached the end of Jesus' discourse in Matthew 13. This is the conclusive remark. Jesus' parable came from what he observed daily at the lake of Galilee (also known as the Sea of Galilee). Fishermen usually cast a very wide (probably as wide as 900 feet sometimes) dragnet into the deeper part of the water and then have two boats drag the net in while gathering fish of all kinds. Perhaps this is why we find Jesus calling fishermen in groups because they worked in partnership to drag a net of fish. After fishermen landed on the shore, they continued to pull the net until the net came fully on shore. When the fish came on shore, they came in all sizes and species. Most were quite edible by today's standard. Why would Jesus have a separation of good fish and bad fish? What made a fish good or bad?

When reading this simple story, we must remember that Matthew wrote in light of Jewish laws. The Old Testament passage Lev 11:9–12 lists criteria for bad fish: fish that had no fins or scales. Some think that Matthew 13 has Old Testament imagery associated with God allowing Babylon to catch Judeans like fish (Hab. 14-17).[1] Still, purity laws make more sense. The fish themselves were not morally bad, but its badness came from purity laws. Fishermen were not Hebrew Bible scholars, but ritual purity had been so ingrained in their society that they inevitably had to sort out the fish. The Greek word for "bad" means something like "reprehensible" or "rotten." Probably there would not have been too many dead and rotten fish floating on the surface of the water to warrant the fishermen to sit down and sort them out. Greedy fishermen would have tried to sell the entire catch of fish to the society of gentiles and Jews, with no consideration of ritual purity.

---

1. Snodgrass, *Stories with Intent*, 488.

Ritual purity had so restricted Jewish economics that Jesus and the Gospel writers would often condemn the rich because of the many who would earn extra money without regard for any law. For non-Jewish fishermen, almost the entire crop of fish was profitable and acceptable for business. They never stopped to consider whether some fish were ritually unclean because ritual concern never existed in their minds. The Jewish requirement, on the other hand, would have been stringent in comparison to the way we eat fish today. For example, where I grew up in the southern part of the US, people regularly eat catfish. At the lake of Galilee, there were also catfish. Such a fish would not have been sold among Jews because no one would eat it. The fish was not evil; only ritually impure. After all, fish have no morals.

The next part of the parable, the concluding part, only fits when we read the above story about fishing in light of the Old Testament, because Jesus points to the teacher of the law in 13:52.

Jesus continued to talk about the expert in the law in 13:51–52. This is an extremely difficult saying at the end, partly because it has no exact parallel in the Gospels and partly because it does not cohere with the context above. It is easy to see this as some kind of addition by Matthew, but no matter how we see the source of this saying, it needs an explanation in light of the discussion above. The entire saying should be related to "these things" in 13:51. What are these things? They are the summary of all that was taught, not just the teaching about the treasure, the pearl, and the fish. These things would include the ministry of the word from the sower parable in 13:3–23, the mixed community of faith in 13:24–30, the humble beginning of the kingdom that impacted the vast mission in 13:31–35, the preciousness (and care) for the kingdom in 13:44–46, and the final judgment of the kingdom in 13:47–50. Interestingly, the growth parables related to plants are all organic. In other words, the organic aspect is a bit unpredictable and even unconventional. Nevertheless, growth would happen, if the kingdom were given time. These things, then, started at the inception of the kingdom and continued to its culmination. These things would represent the way Jesus saw history. History was a linear progression towards God's judgment. It was revealed through the Law and the Prophets.

The experts in the law who had become kingdom citizens now would not have to sacrifice the old for the new. What then was the "old?" Based on Matthew 13 here, the old would represent that value system coming from the Law, such as purity laws from the fish parable. The word "old" means "antiquated." The word "new" means "unprecedented." The new would probably represent what such ritual laws actually show about God through Jesus' words and, later, deeds. Jesus showed unprecedented words and deeds. Who then were the experts of the law to whom Jesus referred here? We cannot avoid seeing a negative connotation in "expert in the law" if we base our understanding on Matthew's usage. In Jesus' society (as well as Matthew's), the scribes held authoritative positions and served as scriptural gatekeepers. In Matthew, they were often Jesus' enemies (e.g., 9:3).

In order to appreciate the powerful position of the scribe, we have to consider the situation a long time before Jesus. During the time of Ezra, the returning exiles had tried their best to recover the spirit of obedience to the law. Since the entire returnee governance had to be based on interpretation and applications of ancient laws, scribes would naturally gain powerful positions. Their position remained quite powerful even in the Sanhedrin, the Jewish governing body in Jesus' time, simply because they continued to be the interpreters who helped religious leaders govern. Jesus in Matt 23:2–7 recognized their prominent role even in his own society. While their teachings were often quite full of truth (23:3a), some had enjoyed their accolades a bit too much (23:5–6). In Jesus' time, some would behave like some prominent modern pastors who insist repeatedly that people call them "doctor" instead of the usual "reverend," "pastor," or the apparently lowly "brother" or "sister." At the same time, Matthew's Jesus condemned such people roundly for their hypocrisy (15:7–9; 23:3, 13–33), which resulted in their becoming internally impure (15:11, 16–20).

Is it possible for the experts in the law to learn the ways of God's kingdom through Jesus? The experts in the law here probably may mean either the scribes who would follow Jesus eventually or as another way of describing the disciples who learned from Jesus in order to understand the real truth about God. The word for the English phrase "has been trained" can also be translated "has been discipled" or "instructed." This terminology in Matthew denotes discipleship (cf. 28:19). Thus, Matthew's Jesus, in this rare instance, described a possibility of a scribe becoming a disciple and using the old and new to teach others. If the second meaning is Jesus' term, then Jesus was talking about himself like the new law teacher and lawgiver, like Moses, teaching the true Israelites about God's will. By this saying about scribes turned kingdom citizens, Matthew's Jesus kept consistency with earlier teachings regarding the law (e.g., 5:17–48). The new came from the old. When Jesus blended the old and the new together, the real expert in the law would be one who would accept both. The one who accepted only the old while rejecting the new would be the traditionalist who was not only unworthy to teach for the kingdom but also unacceptable for the final judgment depicted in the fish parable. In other words, Jesus' teaching about the kingdom was not baseless. It had an old origin that would demonstrate renewal in Israel. The new kingdom disciple-scribe would then contrast against the other scribes whom Jesus condemned in Matt 23. A question remains. How was the trained scribe of the kingdom like the owner of the house who brought out old and new treasures out of the storehouse?

This is a tough question to ask and even tougher to answer. The answer has to be open-ended. We must be quite careful not to allegorize the house to be some kind of symbol of the scribe's heart. After all, the scribe was like the owner. He could not be both the owner and the house. The house was not the scribe. The owner of the house could bring out such treasures for examination and study, or for display. The most important thing about bringing out the old and the new was the preciousness of both. A trained scribe, like the owner of the house, would treat both as treasure to be examined or displayed.

The conclusion about the scribe really is the conclusion of this entire parable segment because it begins with "then" in 13:52. What Jesus taught here probably should be considered new. The idea behind the scribe conclusion is parallel with the separation of the fish. The conclusion about the scribe also points to a separation between old and new while the fishing story also talks about separation of the bad and the good. In a highly logical and ironic sequence, Jesus basically was describing the good and bad scribe. The good scribe would be separated for the kingdom while the bad would receive his punishment. The good one, ironically, would not separate the old from the new. Much like the ritually clean or unclean fish, the separation of good scribe versus the bad scribe had less to do with ritual cleanliness but had everything to do with dealing with Jesus' teachings.

Part of the reason why I told the story backwards without throwing away the "bad" fish is because many times, people did keep a lot of the fish to maximize profit, even in Jesus' day. Many gentiles still ate ritually unclean fish. Many Jewish fishermen would not have cared because they really wanted to earn a bigger profit. In contrast, the kingdom Jesus talked about was legally selective. The kingdom had standards. The fishing method Jesus talked about was exclusively Jewish, when the fishermen spent so much time separating good ones from bad ones. It was consistent with the way

God revealed himself in the Torah. Thus, the message of Jesus' parable fit perfectly into God's salvation history. The ritually unclean were judged harshly in Jesus' day. Certainly, the wicked and the righteous in 13:49 were moral categories of human beings related to legal legislation of the Old Testament law, the Bible Jesus read. The coming judgment God would bring resembled the way Jews separated clean from unclean. The ritual laws in the Torah then acted as an analogy to God's way of salvation. If the story were told backward the way I did earlier, the whole scenario would have changed. Due to the fact that this parable follows the explanation of the wheat and weeds parable, the discussion about judgment would not have worked at all to support the eschatological parable of 13:36–43. In fact, for Matthew's Jesus, inclusion of all the fish would implicate the character of divine judgment itself, going against the very divine nature revealed in the ritual laws. Jesus then pointed out the essence of ritual laws as a means of revelation about God's judgment based on a standard of purity and impurity, but not in terms of rituals but in terms of accepting the kingdom in the way Jesus laid out the teaching in Matt 13. The violent ending for the bad fish in 13:50 resembles 13:42. Such rhetorical violence, as Crossan points out, is commonplace and continues three more times in Matthew (22:13; 24:51; 25:30).[2] Its purpose is no doubt to put the gravity of the matter in the most serious terms imaginable.

PUTTING THE TEXT IN HISTORY: MEANINGS FOR THE WORLD OF AUTHOR-READERS

The biggest tension this series of stories creates for Matthew is its strong implications for the Roman imperial society. Matthew's Jesus claimed strongly that history had a meaning. Its meaning was not to be found in the greater conquest of Rome. Neither was it in the territorial upkeep of the great empire. Nor was it about the restoration of the nation of Israel, necessarily.

The religious tension in Matthew's faith community with the synagogue institution of Judaism is unmistakable. Jesus mentioned the scribe. In such a community, scribes held much power, as the only thing they could preserve now (after the temple destruction) was God's word. Matthew's Jesus made important contribution to the present discussion. Negatively, Matthew's audience learned that divine judgment would be based on

2. Crossan, *The Power of Parable*, 190–191.

separation between the clean and the unclean, presumably with the clean being followers of Jesus. The corporate identity of each group would be quite clearly separated, both presently and in the eschaton. Positively, even though the scribes in Matthew generally despised Jesus, Jesus opened the way for them to adopt the new while preserving the old in the kingdom. Matthew's community needed scribes. Jesus' saying invited them into Matthew's community. If fish represented humans, then Matthew was fishing for new Christ-following scribes (cf. 4:19).

Matthew's portrait of the scribal saying is interesting in that it did several things to its audience. First, it provided an apologetic for Jesus who, in Matthew's opinion, did not abandon the old. Second, it polemicized against the traditionalist whose main mentality was to preserve the old. The real kingdom identity was in both the old and the new, with each part in its Christocentric place.

In the developed world, churches have become architectural wonders. When people say, "I'm going to church," they mean the building. Many churches continue to cultivate the obsession to build bigger buildings, and to house bigger programs, in order to invite more people. Somewhere along the way buildings, rather than people, become the focus. Tradition, rather than truth, became the mainstay. Other churches have prominent members who see their role to be the running of the church and the preservation of their power. Their sense of belonging long ago evolved into full ownership. The church is "their church" instead of "God's church." Such obsession with the temporary is not limited to large churches. Small churches can also suffer the same illness. These parables have something to say about this unhealthy obsession with the "here and now."

The parable of the fish speaks directly to our modern worldview. It speaks of something greater than the "here and now." It speaks of judgment and the final chapters of history where nothing anyone hoards will matter. It speaks uncomfortably about separation between the pure and the impure. It affirms the kingdom's end of 13:30, where those who belong to the kingdom will be separated from those who do not. If this parable is based on purity law, then Jesus spoke about purity in terms of something greater than rituals. Instead, he spoke of yielding crop in 13:23. Jesus then would encourage the modern follower not to love this world so much that the goal of history is no longer in sight. Without considering the linear history of salvation, the modern believer might continue to hoard as if this life is all that matters.

Regarding the faith community, Matthew's Jesus was not mainly concerned with how large our church buildings are or how organized our religious institutions are. If believers live as if numbers matters that much to God, they are living out my backward retelling of the parable. In the retelling of the parable, the focus is all about numbers. Jesus' focus is the crop born by faith communities large and small. The separation of the fish at the end would be based upon this inner purity, which ought to mark the community members. Therefore, each faith community ought to go after the mission of helping their members produce righteous works compatible with the seed sown by the sower. Once again, the message essentially says, "Choose righteousness so that the seed was not sown in vain." The seed was sown with the goal of renewal so that when history comes to pass, the good fish would remain. When God is in charge (i.e., kingdom of heaven), history's meaning will become clear as it progresses towards its goal. When the faith community sees history in those terms, it no longer focuses only on the temporary, superficial, and visible.

This passage is not easy to preach mainly because it is the ending of a series of parables. Apart from those parables, this passage means so much less. In other words, this parable can be preached by itself, but the preacher must interpret based on the preceding parables. It does not only conclude all the parables, but also provides a conclusion about how history will play out in light of Jesus' ministry. The suggested outline is as follows.

Title: Separating the Bad from the Good
Telling It Backward: Profit always trumps everything . . . but the kingdom is not like that. Is more always better?

1) The catch (13:47)
2) The separation (13:48)
3) The moral (13:49–52)
Conclusion: the bad fish (the scribe who rejected the new), the good fish (the scribe who accepted both the old and the new). Separation decreases the number of usable fish. No, more is not better.

REFLECTION QUESTIONS

1. Why did the fish get separated?

2. What would mark bad fish from good fish?

3. What is the meaning of the expert in the law?

4. Why did Jesus all of a sudden bring up the expert in the law?

5. What portrait did Matthew paint of Jesus by talking about the old and the new? Why?

6. What view of history was Matthew's Jesus promoting?

7. How does Jesus' fish parable and view of history implicate the individual believer and the faith community?

6

Relationship or Transaction?

TELLING IT BACKWARD: MATTHEW 18:10-14

> Jesus told this parable: "If someone owns a hundred sheep and
> one of them goes astray, will he not leave the ninety-nine on the
> mountains and go look for the one that went astray? No, he will
> not because losing only one is far better than putting the ninety-
> nine at risk from being left by themselves."

PART OF BEING IN business is about risk management. Sometimes business
suffers losses. There is a saying "cut your losses." It means the person who
loses decides to lose small in order to save the bigger parts that are not yet
lost. The art of cutting losses is about prioritization in a less-than-best situation. The entire endeavor makes business sense. Many would choose the
sensible choice of this backward story. Yet, neither Jesus nor Matthew told
the story this way. In fact, Jesus seems to be saying the opposite.

TELLING IT NORMAL: KEY ELEMENTS IN THE STORY

> 10 "See that you do not disdain one of these little ones. For I tell
> you that their angels in heaven always see the face of my Father in
> heaven. 12 What do you think? If someone owns a hundred sheep
> and one of them goes astray, will he not leave the ninety-nine on
> the mountains and go look for the one that went astray? 13 And if
> he finds it, I tell you the truth, he will rejoice more over it than over

the ninety-nine that did not go astray. 14 In the same way, your
Father in heaven is not willing that one of these little ones be lost."

The story began not at 18:10. Rather, it began at 18:1. The main issue is
quite clear. The main issue arises from the question in 18:1, "Who is the
greatest in the kingdom?" Jesus used a very straightforward logic to give the
answer. First, he did not say immediately that the child was the greatest, but
those who became humble like the child would be the greatest (18:2–4). The
word "humble" can also translate as "made low." Jesus used a future tense to
describe humility in 18:4 to convey three ideas. First, Jesus considered the
listener more powerful than the young child. Second, Jesus called for a free
choice to lower oneself as a distinct possibility (i.e., by using future tense).
Third, the individual singular "humble himself" shows the choice of humility to be individual choice. No one could make that choice for the disciple.
Such people were willing to lower themselves as if they had a small status
of a child. In other words, people whom Jesus considered truly great were
those who willingly abandon their powerful position (regardless of their
social status) to be in the same plane as the humble child. To illustrate his
lowly position, the child never spoke in the entire story. He was voiceless
both in Matthew's narrative and in that society. In other words, both the
child and those who willingly lowered themselves to the lowest social status
would be numbered among the greatest. Second, how great would such a
child be? Jesus had the answer. Welcoming such a child would be the same
as welcoming Jesus (18:5). Jesus was speaking in hyperbole. After all, how
would such a child be of the same status as Jesus? But the point is clear. The
child had a status that would make welcoming him the same as welcoming
Jesus. Imagine!

Jesus spoke in great hyperbole again as he talked about the seriousness
of stumbling such a little one, calling it equal to looking for a fatal curse
(18:6). The curse would be the equivalent of tying a huge stone to oneself and jumping into the ocean. Jesus then talked about things that would
cause people to stumble including limbs and eyes (18:7–9). The thing many
popular interpreters do not remember about 18:7–9 is that Jesus' saying
about limbs and eyes was analogizing those who stumbled the most important members of the kingdom. In other words, the fate of the cut-off limbs
and gouged-out eyeballs was the same as that of the person who caused
stumbling. Such a person did not value the most important members. In
other words, Jesus was saying, "It is not enough just to identify who the
most important member is. It is equally important that such a member

receives all the necessary protection." Thus, Jesus progressed from "who is it" to "what to do about that person." The subsequent parable is the illustration of all that Jesus had said. First, Jesus had said people ought to realize that the young child was valuable to such a degree that he occupied the privileged position of greatness. Second, the other members were to offer all necessary protection for this child.

By the way I told the parable backward, I have included the business of shepherding. Although the text does not say that the person was a shepherd, I think it is safe to assume this person to be one. Jesus however focused on the absurd version. This flock was a modest size—one hundred sheep was no small flock. The fact that the person knew there were ninety-nine shows that he had taken the time to count each sheep, certainly showing a degree of care. Many commentators just take it for granted that seeking one sheep was the usual practice of Palestinian shepherds, but let us think a little harder. The reality of shepherding was more complicated. Who would leave the ninety-nine sheep for the wolf and robbers to steal? Yet, Jesus asked the question in 18:12 as if searching for the one were normal because he was expecting a "yes" for an answer. An irresponsible and foolish shepherd with no business sense would certainly leave the majority to look for a singular lost sheep. A person who was completely in love with the one sheep would. A person driven by his obsessive impulse rather than sensibility would. To prove my point about the absurdity of the person's emotional state, Jesus did say in 18:13, "He will rejoice more over it than over the ninety-nine that did not go astray."

Now, let us assume the best-case scenario. The person had put his ninety-nine sheep in a protected area first. However, it does not explain reasonably how he would rejoice over one sheep above the other ninety-nine. The ninety-nine needed love too. Jesus' humor is in the shepherd's unrestraint obsession with the one sheep. This shepherd was, humorously and unusually, in love with this one sheep. Jesus was not telling the tale according to the normal societal practice, but depicted an unusual way that went against all logic of business investment. Was that not the point, though?

The above warped logic fits perfectly with the previous story about who the greatest was in the kingdom. Who would think that a child and those who received this legally lowly creature would become the greatest in the kingdom? How in fact would receiving this child be like receiving Jesus in 18:5? Jesus was, after all, the rabbi with social status, but this child was the opposite. Why would such a child afford the greatest protection from stumbling as in 18:7–9? Whatever we believe about personal angels in 18:10, obviously the assignment of angels over children in Jesus' saying shows that these children were indeed important in God's eyes also.[1] The little one was of supreme worth. The abnormal of the society became the norm for Jesus' disciples.

In this parable, Jesus was not saying to throw all common sense out to look for a sheep, but he was describing a kind of obsession the shepherd had with the lost one. This abnormal obsession should be the passion of the church as well. The church's way of dealing with those with low social status (e.g., a child or those with the same humble status) is the indicator of whether the kingdom message is understood. Jesus' parable is as counter-cultural as his teaching prior to it. The parable should not stand by itself, at least not in the way Matthew retold Jesus' story. It serves as an illustration of 18:1–9. In summary, Matthew's Jesus focused on two truths. First, Jesus asked each individual to humble himself/herself through abandoning his/her social status. Second, Jesus asked everyone to protect those with low social status with a radical passion that almost denies logic. Thus, those who had status would willingly abandon it to seek those who had no status.

Many see the parable as a statement about a mission to and rejoicing over a lost sinner. This is not the meaning at all. After all, in 18:6 Jesus said that the little one was a believer. It is about community care and priority. The shepherd story only shows what radical care for the least important person *within* the community looks like. We must notice that Jesus analogized the moral of the story to God's sentiment towards sinners. When the Father in heaven is in charge (i.e., kingdom of heaven), the church would reflect the divine love for the weak and powerless.

PUTTING THE TEXT IN HISTORY: MEANINGS FOR THE WORLD OF AUTHOR-READERS

When we read this strange tale of Matthew's, we need to set it within his society's system. The patron-client value system penetrated every part of society. People depended on the powerful to get ahead. In Chinese society, a similar phenomenon occurs to this day. The Chinese call it "gwan shi." The idea of "gwan shi" is made clearer by the American adage "you scratch my back and I'll scratch yours." The way to get ahead is not about what

---

1. In Matthew (e.g., 13:49), angels could have the function of executing judgment.

we know but whom we know. Relationships easily turn into transactions. However, in this parable, when relationship becomes a transaction, it loses its meaning.

When Jesus talked of this parable, he both worked within and outside of the patron-client relationship. When Jesus addressed the disciples, he addressed them as the powerful who needed to watch out for the powerless. Jesus recognized the existing system and addressed the powerful. In so doing, Jesus recognized no quick fix to the system's flaws. Yet, part of the problem should be solved at least to a large extent by turning a shepherding story upside down. The faith community should become the solution rather than a perpetuation of the problem. Matthew used Jesus' warped logic to show how utterly different the attitude of the powerful should be. The attitude would mark the identity of the community.

We have to put this story within the situation of Matthew to see Matthew's radical message. Here, we have to use a little imagination. When the Christ-following Jews separated from the synagogues, they lost quite a lot of power. They still needed to have enough support, both socially and financially, to do well. Their natural tendency would be to lean towards the powerful either from their former connections or towards those who were rich in their community. Revenue generation would seem to be a necessary strategy for survival. Yet, Matthew's Jesus thought quite differently. Matthew exhorted his community to see itself not as victims of alienation from synagogues, but helpers of real victims. Matthew told this community that its obsession ought to be with the lowly even at the risk of endangering the ninety-nine. Surely, Matthew's Jesus was exaggerating, but hyperbole had a way of sending a loud and radical message to its recipients. Matthew then exhorted his community to identify with the lowly, presuming the community itself was made up of the high and mighty. Whether the community saw itself as having a lot of high and mighty people was quite another matter, but Matthew assumed the ninety-nine percent to be the strong. Only one percent was the weak. The strong then existed to serve the weak, not based on economics but purely based on Jesus' kingdom principle of caring for the lowly.

I recall coming back to the US after having been gone for a while studying for my PhD in England. We visited a very large nearby church. We had our two young children with me at the time (around age three and one). In our family, we are in the habit of having our children worship with us in the "big service." Not so this church! The greeters at the door firmly told us that we needed to bring our children to their respective children's programs. Upon further inquiry, they assured us that little children making noise would bother the preacher. Besides, the children had to be ordered to their own program so that the church could accommodate more adults. Yes, this is what they told me. This philosophy goes directly against the simplest and plainest understanding of Jesus' teaching about the lost sheep. Children are not numbers. Seats in the church (or even membership in the kingdom) are not for sale. When society's standard of organization takes over the organism that is the church, we are at great risk of losing the essentials of the kingdom. Worse yet, the church chooses the backward story where the ninety-nine become more important.

Broader than the issue of children is the formation of a faith community, according to Matthew. Matthew's ideal about the identity of the faith community was a radical embrace not of the powerful ninety-nine but the powerless one. The radicalness of the embrace would be so strong that, at times, it would seem illogical. When we talk of power and humility, we are talking about social-political realities. The powerful, who have generated power from politics and money (often with the two being linked together), control the powerless. Many segments of our church actually advocate values and worldviews of the powerful instead of the powerless. The Christian Right's endorsement of Nixon has already taught us that powerful public figures who lend us their power, albeit temporarily, can cost us dearly. Yet, this painful lesson continues to elude many. I have seen both church leaders and even theologians continue to court the powerful not only privately but also publicly in writing. They are living out the backward telling of the parable. The real parable, instead, tells us to embrace those who are powerless, and God would be pleased. Matthew was making both missional and social-political statements here. His Jesus meant for us to form our community identity based on his teachings. The greatest do not come from societal appearance of greatness. The greatest are the weak and those who minister among them. So are those who will humble themselves like a child (18:4). The parable essentially proclaims, "Choose Jesus' kind of greatness over the world's greatness."

For preachers who wish to preach this passage, the essential question of greatness must stand out in the sermon. If we do so inductively, we can bring up the essential question in 18:1 at the conclusion, and not at the beginning. Who we think is the greatest says much about our identity as kingdom citizens. The following can be a sample outline.

Title: When Greatness is Radical
Telling It Backward: The ninety-nine are precious for profit . . .
but the kingdom is not like that. Is the kingdom about profit?

1) Irrational favoring of the one (18:10–14)
2) The key reason: 18:1
Conclusion: The main difference—relationships are not a transaction when the little one is the most important member. The kingdom is not about profit but about illogical love for its greatest member, the little one.

REFLECTION QUESTIONS

1. What if the shepherd only cared about his investment?

2. How is the way Jesus told the story strange?

3. What was the social status of a child like in Jesus' day?

4. What is the importance of the singular "humble himself?"

5. Reflect on what anti-kingdom value our society teaches in light of this parable.

7

A Community of Honesty, Repentance, Forgiveness, and Reconciliation

TELLING IT BACKWARD: MATTHEW 18:21–35

Then Peter came to him and said, "Lord, how many times must I forgive my brother who sins against me? As many as seven times?" Jesus said to him, "Not seven times, I tell you, but seventy-seven times!

"For this reason, the kingdom of heaven is like a king who wanted to settle accounts with his slaves. As he began settling his accounts, a man who owed ten thousand talents was brought to him. Because he was not able to repay it, the lord ordered him to be sold, along with his wife, children, and whatever he possessed, and repayment to be made. Then the slave threw himself to the ground before him, saying, 'Be patient with me, and I will repay you everything.' The lord had compassion on that slave and released him, and forgave him the debt. After he went out, that same slave found one of his fellow slaves who owed him one hundred silver coins. After the slave demanded from his fellow slave the one hundred silver coins, his fellow slave threw himself down and begged him, 'Be patient with me, and I will repay you.' The first debtor had compassion on that slave and released him, and forgave him the debt. Forgive because your heavenly Father has forgiven you."

THE WAY I TOLD this above story seems to fall in line with the forgiveness theme Jesus attempted to teach, especially addressing Peter's question of "how many times." It does teach the positive side of forgiveness; that since the master had forgiven a servant, the servant must also forgive others who owe them less than he owed his master. My telling of the story seems to have done the job. Yet, neither Jesus nor Matthew told the story in the above fashion. Jesus told a story with a stronger edge.

TELLING IT NORMAL: KEY ELEMENTS IN THE STORY

21 Then Peter came to him and said, "Lord, how many times must I forgive my brother who sins against me? As many as seven times?" 22 Jesus said to him, "Not seven times, I tell you, but seventy-seven times!

23 "For this reason, the kingdom of heaven is like a king who wanted to settle accounts with his slaves. 24 As he began settling his accounts, a man who owed ten thousand talents was brought to him. 25 Because he was not able to repay it, the lord ordered him to be sold, along with his wife, children, and whatever he possessed, and repayment to be made. 26 Then the slave threw himself to the ground before him, saying, 'Be patient with me, and I will repay you everything.' 27 The lord had compassion on that slave and released him, and forgave him the debt. 28 After he went out, that same slave found one of his fellow slaves who owed him one hundred silver coins. So he grabbed him by the throat and started to choke him, saying, 'Pay back what you owe me!' 29 Then his fellow slave threw himself down and begged him, 'Be patient with me, and I will repay you.' 30 But he refused. Instead, he went out and threw him in prison until he repaid the debt. 31 When his fellow slaves saw what had happened, they were very upset and went and told their lord everything that had taken place. 32 Then his lord called the first slave and said to him, 'Evil slave! I forgave you all that debt because you begged me! 33 Should you not have shown mercy to your fellow slave, just as I showed it to you?' 34 And in anger his lord turned him over to the prison guards to torture him until he repaid all he owed. 35 So also my heavenly Father will do to you, if each of you does not forgive your brother from your heart."

Once, someone told me, "If you want to lend money to a friend, just consider it a gift or your friendship will be ruined." Relationships frequently get broken when someone owes another something because of the unequal power relationship of debt. Jesus' answer to Peter using a parable about lending is full of insight because it did not merely deal with forgiveness but uneven distribution of power. This unevenness can cause great headaches.

In order to understand this parable, we have to look at the context. The passage of Matt 18:15–20 explains 18:21–35. Let us just summarize the issue by looking briefly at the plot of 18:15–20. The passage of 18:15–20 often get misunderstood because of its conclusion being read as a promise for prayer meetings. In Jesus' day, it had nothing to do with prayer meetings. It had everything to do with conflicts between community members. Already, in 18:1–14, Jesus had taught about the importance of first becoming a person of the lowliest status and second becoming passionate about loving a child or anyone whose status was equally lowly. With that humility and passionate love, Jesus' teaching could have ended, and everything would have been satisfactory. Clearly, Jesus thought that human conflicts within the community could not be solved merely by humility, though humility ought to be part of the picture. More important should be the tension between individual piety in the previous context (e.g., 18:4) and corporate relationships here.

Jesus dealt with the church in the present situation. Matthew is the only Gospel that used the word "church" so extensively (16:18). The word for "church" was originally used for assembly. If we compare the present passage with 16:17–19, the connection between the faith community at the time of Jesus and the future community would become clearer. The nature of this assembly was at once present in Jesus' setting and future in Matthew's community. Within Jesus' setting, it would have been a religious gathering, as he used Greek vocabulary descriptive of the synagogue in 18:20. Jesus was worried about the community relationships of his disciples. Jesus was not concerned with easy forgiveness. Rather, he wanted brothers to confront each other honestly but with a big dose of grace, knowing that two or three witnesses who gathered to deal with this situation would have been ultimately responsible to Jesus (18:20). The community's authority had to be exercised with caution. Like the previous teaching on the little one, Jesus assumed here that the community of disciples held the power.

In the above context of 18:15–20, the parable demonstrates fully the kind of power relationship Jesus wanted to teach. Peter himself, who asked the question, surely would have seen the power relationship in forgiveness. The fact that he could ask "how many times" shows the forgiver having the power to withhold or dispense forgiveness. For Peter, forgiveness had limits. The person who could set the limit would be the one holding all the power. Instead of withholding the power, Jesus told Peter to release it through forgiveness—not just seven times, but seventy-seven times or, as some translations have it, seventy times seven. The figure of seven offered by Peter denoted the number of perfection in Jesus' society. The number Jesus used surpassed all societal ethical standards. Here comes the story.

The story divides into three simple scenes. The entire story is the illustration of all that Jesus said about forgiveness because Jesus started with "for this reason" before he unfolded the story. First, in 18:23–27, Jesus told of the interaction between the king and the slave who owed him. For some strange reason, this slave owed the king a fortune. The amount in Greek can be translated "myriads of talents." "Talent" was a weight of a certain coin. The Greek expresses something like a "humongous amount." One commentator states starkly, "10,000 talents is Bill Gates' kind of money."[1] It is the largest amount the Greek numbering system can express. The amount, for the ordinary peasant, would be impossible to repay. Jesus always had a knack for the dramatic, by characterizing the man as a slave and his lord (or master) a king whose social status could not have been greater. Obviously, Jesus' story was completely fictional. The likelihood of a slave being able to borrow this much money and squandering was near impossible. Was the king an idiot? Nevertheless, the impossibly large amount was possible in this parable because Jesus was trying to make a point.

As if the contrasting status of a king and slave was not enough, Jesus also called the king "the lord," denoting some kind of obligation from the slave. The slave was in real trouble. Since he was not able to repay, the lord was going to sell the slave's wife and children, and all that he had to get some payment in 18:25. This would leave the slave with absolutely nothing. Such a story illustrates the possibility of this kind of cruelty among gentiles because Jews did not sell the family members of each other.[2] The slave, knowing that he was in deeper trouble than almost anyone he knew, kneeled down to beg in 18:26. The lord took pity and erased his debt.

This brings us to the second part of the parable in 18:28–30. Here the first debtor, the slave, went to find a fellow slave who owed him about one hundred day's wages. In 20:2, a denarius was one day's wage. The New English Translation is correct to translate it "one hundred silver coins." Some

---

1. Brosend, *Conversations with Scripture*, 61.
2. Snodgrass, *Stories with Intent*, 66.

translations have footnotes of "a few dollars" which is an underestimation. The first debtor's initial reaction was violence, demanding his money back. Since the second debtor could not repay the debt, the first debtor threw him into prison until he would pay back the one hundred silver coins. How did a slave have that much money to lend to a fellow slave? Two possibilities existed. First, he could have used some of the king's money to lend to a fellow slave as an investment. Second, he could have saved some of the pocket money all slaves were given in Roman society.

This brings us to the third part of the parable in 18:31–34. The third part of the story in 18:31–34 contains mainly the outcry from the other slaves. Apparently, the other slaves did not like what the first debtor did and reported to the lord. Once again, Jesus used "lord" to emphasize the legal status of the king over his slaves. The expectation seems to be mercy for the second debtor since the lord forgave the first debtor. The end result was the jailing of the first debtor who would experience torture until he should pay back all the money he owed.

Jesus concluded his saying in 18:35, saying that this would be the way the heavenly Father would treat each of Jesus' followers who chose not to forgive his or her brothers (and sisters) from the heart. Matthew recorded Jesus' last saying as a mixture of singular and plurals. This mixture may be noteworthy or maybe just a stylistic variation. Matthew recorded what the heavenly Father would do to "you" (in plural), only to use the singular "each of you" to describe the process of forgiveness. Maybe Matthew used the plural to denote a general condition while using the singular to show the individual decision involved. The singular "brother" also shows each singular case needing this decision. Matthew ended with "from your hearts" in plural for both "your" and "hearts," showing once again no exception being made. The word for forgiveness actually means "to release." A release fits the whole parable of being released from one's debt and imprisonment or punishment.

Forgiveness does not denote that the hurt was any less painful, but it has to do with releasing the debtor from his obligations of reparation. The decision had to be made by the victim, specifically when the victim held powerful sway over the debtor. This raises the question of whether this is universally applicable, or whether Jesus was talking about the specific case of the powerful being wronged by the less powerful. Peter's problem was about repeated trespasses only because the less powerful could afford to trespass against the one who holds the power. I propose that both Peter's question and Jesus' answer were talking about specific power relationship instead of merely forgiveness in general.

When reading the entire story, we may notice certain repeated phrases. 18:26 and 18:29 are basically the same with the debtors begging on their knees. Jesus painted a picture of desperate repentance. The result however could not have been more different between the first and second cases. Jesus meant to build this story pattern in order to show the contrast between the first and second cases. The first contrast is the amount of money owed. In 18:24, the first debtor owed several mountains of debt worth several fortunes of several lifetimes. He would find it impossible to repay the debt. In 18:28, the second debtor owed one hundred denarii. The amount, one hundred day's wages, was no small sum but was not impossible. The second contrast is between how the lord treated the first debtor and how the first debtor treated the second debtor. While it would take an eternity to repay the lord, the lord immediately dismissed in a moment's mercy the first debtor's bill. While it might take a short while for the second debtor to repay the first debtor, the first debtor, instead of showing a moment of grace or even a prolonged grace period, showed immediate cruelty.

The story, when Jesus told it, made one outstanding point: its extreme absurdity. The extreme positions between the king and the slave show the impossibility of such a story. Jesus' teaching was talking about accomplishing the impossible in the kingdom through this impossible parable. Peter was contemplating the highest possibility, but Jesus was talking about the *impossible* possibility. The extremely absurd difference between the amount owed to the king and the second amount only highlights the gap between how much Peter owed to God versus how much other trespassers owed Peter. The debt the disciples owed to the powerful God would never compare to what the trespassers owed to them. The different amount shows also how rich and powerful the king was in comparison to the wealth of the slave. When God is in charge (i.e., kingdom of heaven), his followers will realize more and more how impossible God's grace is. The theme of punishment hints are eschatological judgment. Peter's problem was that he focused on the "here and now." Jesus' focus was on how present relationship would impact the eschatological judgment.

I originally told the story backward because the story could go several different ways. If we follow the repeated gesture of the begging debtors, the forgiveness should have soon followed. Since forgiveness was expected, the story would follow the same repeated plot. Certainly, the other fellow slaves expected forgiveness to be given. It seems however, that someone could object by saying that the second debtor's money was not tied to the lord's, but if we follow Jesus' logic closely, all the money the first debtor also owed to the lord's would include the money the second debtor owed to the first debtor. If the second debtor could repay the first debtor, the first debtor would then have enough money to pay back the lord partially.

When reading this parable, much of its meaning ought to relay back to 18:15–20. We have already set the scene of 18:15–20. Thus, obligations accumulated for the first debtor. I shall discuss more about the relevant meaning this parable has today when I discuss preaching below.

PUTTING TEXT IN HISTORY: MEANINGS FOR THE WORLD OF AUTHOR-READERS

Matthew's assembly faced challenging times. The faith community was in the midst of a slow split from synagogues. One of the problems that came along with the formation of this new community was alienation. Inevitably, people took sides. More importantly, some could not make up their minds. Many would stumble and go back to old ways. Others created dissent within the community due to their own idiosyncrasies. In such difficult situations, many relational tensions arose. This parable addressed such tensions. The basis for forgiveness within the community was surely the greater trespass the kingdom citizen had against the creator. The comparison between human sin against God versus sin against one another seems to create an impossible gap. Apparently, the kingdom was this radical. Its radicalness came directly from divine forgiveness. The servant failed to forgive because he really did not appreciate how much he actually owed to the king in comparison to the amount his fellow servant owed him. Repentance and the resulting forgiveness ought to be kingdom traits.

If we survey all the quotes on the internet on bitterness and forgiveness, inevitably many of them focus on the human dimension especially at the individualistic level. Quite often, the logic goes something like this: Many times, bitterness or failure to forgive hurts the victim more than the victimizer because while the bitterness eats at the victim, the victimizer hardly notices. Certainly, that logic has a lot of wisdom and truth, but it is not the whole truth. In Jesus' society, the problem went deeper because if the bitter person held the power, forgiveness became something that worked to the advantage of the powerful. So, if the victim were powerful, the victimizer would be in deep trouble.

When looking at forgiveness in terms of power, the victim held the power to release the bitterness. This seems very unfair and feels less satisfying. Yet, Jesus pointed at the justice of God as the basis. The victim is never without sin. He or she also trespasses against a greater lord, the heavenly Father. Thus, trespasses are always viewed in terms of relative degree. The only one holding all the power is God. The forgiving person recognizes and trusts in divine justice and power. The forgiving person also allows for delayed justice.

This parable is not that difficult to preach in its simplistic fashion, but pastorally, it deserves much more sensitivity. Many have suffered deep hurts in the past. I have heard about a case of mishandled preaching of the parable. The pastor at the end encouraged all victims to imagine in their minds the victimizers and mentally release them. Trouble with this approach pastorally is that the victim's imagination got re-victimized. Literally, some of the congregation had nightmares the following week, due to severe sexual abuse cases. This instance is an example of how not to preach the parable. In fact, the preacher had mistakenly put the entire responsibility on the victims. We shall see below that this approach is neither Jesus nor Matthew's approach. Instead of being a place of healing, the church can be a place where victims suffer twice.

Victimhood is a complex issue, often made simplistic by religious and pietistic people. I read one article with a part of its title saying "seventy times seven? I can barely forgive some corrupt clergy once."[3] The greatest injury often comes from those closest to us or from those we put on the pedestal. Exegetically, the parable is not merely saying that the victim has power, because the victim rarely has power. We need to ask how the victim would gain any power to forgive. The power resides in the community of believers within 18:15–20. The community could bind and release in 18:18. Thus, the community had the obligation to stand on the side of the victim.

Contrary to popular understanding of this parable, Jesus' teaching was not about unconditional forgiveness. Neither was it the last resort because retaliation was not an option, as some people seem to think. Even if we apply 18:15–17 legalistically, Jesus' forgiveness was situational for sure. Jesus clearly described the trespasser being confronted. In other words, before forgiveness could happen, a confrontation (perhaps not only with the

3. Scheller, "How Far Should Forgiveness Go?" 40–44.

victim but also in the presence of two to three people from the community) had to take place. If the person listened, s/he would then release the power of forgiveness to the victim, much like the way the debtor kneeled before the master, but not without the witness and backing of the community. At that point, the victim could choose to forgive. In other words, originally the victimizer held all the power, but by admitting to the trespass, the victim then received the power from the victimizer.

Jesus was not advocating an unconditional or cheap forgiveness. Peter's question arose out of the situation of 18:15–20. Thus, preachers need to face the contextual consideration and set limits on the kind of forgiveness Jesus referred to. Jesus' teaching was not made in a vacuum or abstraction. In other words, Jesus made exact parallel between the teaching about forgiveness in 18:15–20 and the parable, where the trespasser threw himself at the mercy of the person wronged. The kind of forgiveness Jesus talked about was the result of true repentance and giving up of power. Only when power is given up would the space for forgiveness become possible. When God is in charge (i.e., kingdom of heaven), the faith community must choose a holistic approach that leads to forgiveness and reconciliation. In the eschaton, this community would come away with a positive judgment because of its reconciliatory relationships.

One of the biggest success stories of recent time is South Africa. The Anglican Church was involved in the healing process that did not involve easy forgiveness. The victimizers had to confess their wrongdoings. This process avoided a lot of potential bloodshed. True forgiveness only came in South Africa after the people took seriously the offense the white government had committed against the black people. Without naming the evil, whether it is a debt or some other trespasses, complete forgiveness is impossible. When looking at the matter this way, forgiveness is the result of proper exercise of power within the faith community. When cheap forgiveness is urged, the victim may be re-victimized, leaving the victim further alienated. Thus, kingdom forgiveness puts heavy responsibility on the community. If the community does not reflect the justice of God and its proper use of disciplinary power, true forgiveness cannot happen easily.

A less successful case would be the cover-up of sexual abuses in the Roman Catholic Church where many victims still feel bitter. The same can also happen within the Protestant circle. I have seen a recent case in Hong Kong where a young lady was sexually assaulted by another Christian businessman in Taiwan on a business trip. She consulted her spiritual elder who suggested that she should neither report to the police nor confront the rapist. Meanwhile, the rapist returned to Hong Kong. Very soon, she found out that Taiwan has no international extradition agreement with Hong Kong, and she had missed her chance to bring the rapist to justice. Meanwhile, many in the church, including her spiritual elder, still advise her to forgive, since there is nothing she can do now. This grave miscarriage of justice remains a huge blot in the Hong Kong Christian community even today. The faith community and her spiritual elder have failed her. Rather than helping the victim, these people chose silence. Meanwhile, a rapist is running loose in the faith community unpunished, with all his power intact, ready to do more damage. These are the cases we should keep in mind when we preach the parable. Put the responsibility on the community, and not the victim. Since this is a kingdom story with a king, it is teaching not just individuals how to behave as citizens but also the entire kingdom in how to carry out responsibility.

Title: Cheap Forgiveness?
Telling It Backward: The forgiven slave forgives his fellow slave . . . but real-world forgiveness is not always like this. What if forgiveness is impossible?

1) The powerful king and the powerless slave (18:23–27)
2) The powerless slave and the more powerless slave (18:28–30)
3) The king's verdict (18:31–35)
Conclusion: the real deal (18:15–18)—a community should use power wisely to bring repentance and forgiveness. Forgiveness is most possible with the community's help.

REFLECTION QUESTIONS

1. What contrasts did Jesus' parable bring?

2. What do the contrasting amounts of debt in the parable teach about forgiveness?

3. What danger does the parable pose if we only teach the parable?

4. How does power function in the community and in individual victims?

8

Fairness in the Kingdom?

TELLING IT BACKWARD: MATTHEW 20:1–16

Jesus told this parable: "For the kingdom of heaven is like a land-owner who went out early in the morning to hire workers for his vineyard. And after agreeing with the workers for the standard wage of one denarius he sent them into his vineyard. When it was about nine o'clock in the morning, he went out again and saw others standing around in the marketplace without work. He said to them, 'You go into the vineyard too, and I will give you whatever is right.' So they went. When he went out again about noon and three o'clock that afternoon, he did the same thing. And about five o'clock that afternoon he went out and found others standing around, and said to them, 'Why are you standing here all day without work?' They said to him, 'Because no one hired us.' He said to them, 'You go and work in the vineyard too.' When it was evening, the sun was about to set and no more work could be done. The owner of the vineyard said to his manager, 'Call the workers and give the pay starting with the first hired until the last.' And when those hired first came, they received the standard wage of one denarius. When those hired about five o'clock came, each received a only about one hour's worth of pay because, after all, those who worked all day had worked in the burning heat and hardship of the day while these late workers were working in the evening breeze. Whoever comes first will be treated fairly with more and whoever comes last will receive less. That is the fairness of the kingdom of heaven."

THE ABOVE STORYTELLING NEUTRALIZES the unfairness about which these workers complained to the owner. The order of first and last would fit perfectly the sense of justice in Jesus' day. In the backward story above, the sweetness of the labor comes from the fairness of the wages. Every bit of the wage was earned. Nothing would be given away. Everything was exactly fair. Every penny and every drop of sweat were accounted for. Such should be the system for both the ancient and modern world. My backward telling of the parable resolves any tension Jesus' parable causes and creates a nice, neat, and simple system of merit. Yet, neither Jesus nor Matthew told the story this way.

TELLING IT NORMAL: KEY ELEMENTS IN THE STORY

"For the kingdom of heaven is like a landowner who went out early in the morning to hire workers for his vineyard. 2 And after agreeing with the workers for the standard wage, he sent them into his vineyard. 3 When it was about nine o'clock in the morning, he went out again and saw others standing around in the marketplace without work. 4 He said to them, 'You go into the vineyard too, and I will give you whatever is right.' 5 So they went. When he went out again about noon and three o'clock that afternoon, he did the same thing. 6 And about five o'clock that afternoon he went out and found others standing around, and said to them, 'Why are you standing here all day without work?' 7 They said to him, 'Because no one hired us.' He said to them, 'You go and work in the vineyard too.' 8 When it was evening the owner of the vineyard said to his manager, 'Call the workers and give the pay starting with the last hired until the first.' 9 When those hired about five o'clock came, each received a full day's pay. 10 And when those hired first came, they thought they would receive more. But each one also received the standard wage. 11 When they received it, they began to complain against the landowner, 12 saying, 'These last fellows worked one hour, and you have made them equal to us who bore the hardship and burning heat of the day.' 13 And the landowner replied to one of them, 'Friend, I am not treating you unfairly. Didn't you agree with me to work for the standard wage? 14 Take what is yours and go. I want to give to this last man the same as I gave to you. 15 Am I not permitted to do what I want with what belongs to me? Or are you envious because I am generous?' 16 So the last will be first, and the first last."

This is a story that drives everyone crazy. It breaks many conventions and leaves a lot of preachers at a loss for words. Some may want to read it as something "out there" by talking about the differences between modern value and ancient value. Others read it "in the text" by focusing on only the generosity of the owner. Yet, most modern readers would certainly respond in the same way about fairness as those who had come first to work under the landowner. "It is not fair" has probably been shouted across centuries, in spite of cultural differences or the text's supposed claim for the owner's generosity.

The story plot begins easily enough in a typical farming community one early morning (20:1). The amount agreed between the owner and first batch of workers is one day's wage of one denarius (20:2). The second group of workers came in the third hour of the day (20:3). They too got work. The owner appeared to have still more work and needed more workers. So, he went out thrice more, at the sixth, ninth, and eleventh hours (20:5–7). At the end of the day, when the work was done, the last group of workers was paid first with the first workers being paid last (20:8–10). Due to the fact that everyone got equal pay but did not do equal work, the first group of workers who worked the longest had real trouble with this payment scheme (20:11–12). The owner's answer was that the original agreement for payment did not change. Therefore, the owner reserved the right to pay whatever wages he chose (20:13–15). Jesus' final moral of the story was that the last would be first (20:16).

As I have stated above, this story is incredibly difficult to understand because the owner appeared to be a wealthy bully who frustrated any sense of fairness. Within the uneven power relationships of the first century, this present scenario appears to have been quite possible. Another difficulty of this story is the saying Jesus put at the end, as if he endorsed this apparently oppressive system created by the owner. Of course, Jesus did not say, "Go and do likewise," but he came pretty close by suggesting that this is the way things would be in the kingdom, the last being the first and so on. How should we understand this parable? The following discussion will focus on the intricate details of Matthew's (or Jesus') storytelling within the parable first before venturing outside it to include Matthew's narrative context.

The parable plot isolates the first group of workers. In 20:1–2, Jesus only mentioned the amount of daily wages with the first group. Thereafter, Jesus only pointed out that the others were standing around, implying that they were starving of work and of wages (20:3, 6). The repeated idea of standing around versus the amount of pay shows Jesus' emphasis. All the workers would be "standing around" and starving unless the owner chose to call them. The main focus then, was less on the wages and more on the desperate state of affairs for these workers. The implication is that these worker groups, from first to last would be identified as unemployed vagrants unless someone (20:7) such as the owner called them. They all had the same dire fate without the owner. In other words, they were lucky to have been called. It was only after the call that the fairness issue came up.

Jesus' telling of the parable started with the first group of workers and ended with them as well. This unhappy lot made several complaints. They had borne the burden of the work and suffered in the heat while those who came later would not have to work as much and the weather was less harsh at the end of the day. Their action of complaining is also noteworthy. Many translations have "they began to grumble/complain." The tense of the verb could also be translated "they started and continued to grumble." In other words, they were not merely making one little request. They were grumbling continuously until the owner decided to say something about their complaint. Jesus was presenting this group as an annoying bunch of grumblers. The group was complaining, but the owner only addressed a singular worker, perhaps the one who talked the loudest. This singular worker represented the entire group. The owner basically told him that he could pay whatever he wished because he had the rights. Keeping within the context of our previous observation about identity, the owner was basically appealing to the difference of status between himself and those who were called. Those who were called had no rights to begin with, and the owner had all the rights to hire or not to hire. This however does not resolve the problem of the owner being an unfair bully who made use of the patron-client structure of his society to save money. Our present reading does not absolve the owner of his own character flaws. Is this uneven treatment, the first being the last, a kingdom norm?

In order to get this story completely, readers need to read the wider context of Matthew. At the start, 20:1 has a "for." In other words, the entire parable is an explanation of what went on above. The parable itself is inadequate to explain its own meaning. What went on above exactly that requires this strange explanation?

The section 19:16–30 has the story about the rich young man. The real meaning of the vineyard workers in 20:1–16 comes from 19:16–30. Even more self-evident is the pairing of 19:30 with 20:16 with certain minor differences. The differences, though seemingly minor, would reap great interpretive harvest, as later discussion will show. For now, the wider context should inform the interpreter.

Observation of the story's greater context yields the direct relevance of the rich man story to the parable. Let me summarize the story of the rich man, Peter, and Jesus. The rich man came to Jesus asking what he must do to gain eternal life (19:16). What this eternal life consists of is not clear in the story. Jesus' answer to him is to keep the law to gain life, which seems to be a reflection of sections of the Torah that speak about the life that the people of God would gain from Torah-keeping (19:17). There are some important differences between this account and the other Synoptic accounts, but this should not occupy us for our purpose. His answer reflects his propensity to favor some laws over other laws because he asked "Which one?" (19:18). Jesus' answer required maximum obedience. His question to Jesus shows that he wanted selective obedience. Jesus appears to have lured him deeper into a hole, first by stating the basic human relationships from the Decalogue but then demanding that he give up all that he had, give it to the poor, and follow him (19:19–20). Jesus' answer to him shows Jesus' own explanation of what it meant to obey all the commandments. In other words, Jesus wanted to deal with the rest of the stuff the rich man did not want to commit to in order to obey the commandments fully, and in 19:20–21, the rest that he chose not to obey just happened to be his riches. Then Jesus used an analogy to describe how hard it would be for a rich man to go into the kingdom of heaven in 19:23–24. The moral of the story is simple. Because Jesus demanded maximum obedience, the maximum for a rich man was so much more than the poor man, thus making the rich man's entry into the kingdom as tough as camel going through the eye of the needle. Soon enough, the following story about Peter will demonstrate the relevance of this exchange with the rich man.

Jesus turned his attention to the disciples by telling them how hard it would be for a rich man to enter the kingdom (19:23–24). With Jesus' explanation, he clearly points out that gaining eternal life was equal to keeping the Torah, giving everything to the poor, and following him. No wonder, in 19:25–26, the disciples were astonished at the near impossible demands. Jesus told them in 19:26 that for humans, such obedience was impossible but for God, everything was possible. In other words, for the rich man, it would take a divine act to obey in the way Jesus demanded it. This is where Peter popped in, presumably representing the rest of the disciples, and added that the disciples did indeed at least fulfill a part of

Jesus' demand to give up everything and follow him (19:27). Peter followed his answer with a question, "What then will there be for us?" Peter saw the obedience as a kind of bargain. Jesus answered Peter according to Peter's logic that Peter, and all who followed Jesus, would gain much more than they had given up (19:28–29).

When looking at the two exchanges (i.e., exchanges of the rich man and Peter with Jesus), the similarity of logic between the rich man and Peter becomes clear. They both thought that the price paid was very heavy. The difference is the rich man was unwilling and Peter was willing to pay the heavy price. The simple and straightforward plot ends with Jesus' saying about the order of first being last and vise versa (19:30). As the above discussion points out, 19:30 parallels with 20:16. Such a parallel informs interpreters of something much greater at work in the narrative here.

How does the 19:30 and 20:16 pairing inform and reinforce the meaning above? 19:30 seems to show another side of truth that Jesus did not tell Peter because it starts with a "but" while 20:16 features "so" or "in this way" to tell how the first would be last. In other words, 19:30 does not conclude discussion with Peter but transitions to an explanation of a different aspect that Peter needed to learn. The answer Jesus gave to Peter was not single-dimentional, but it was multifaceted. While Peter would be rewarded in Jesus' initial answer to him, Peter also needed to learn not about his own contribution but about his own poverty, much like those people who stood around waiting for work. When dealing with the call of the kingdom, Jesus showed the equal status of every member with every other member. No one was better just because he did more.

The subsequent context in 20:17–28 shows relevance in illuminating the meaning of the parable. The section 20:17–19 talks about Jesus' impending death in Jerusalem. To make matters worse, the mother of Zebedee's sons asked that they would be seated at Jesus' sides in 20:20–21. They clearly did not understand the parable taught earlier and assumed that the worldly system would suit the situation just fine. Jesus seems to be saying that the system was not fine and in many ways opposed to the kingdom value.

One neglected phrase worth mentioning is 20:15 where the Greek literally says something like "Are you giving the evil eye because I am generous?" The idiomatic expression of the eye (translated by Matthew, of course) is telling in that the eye obviously indicated the attitude that comes from a vision of the world. Was not Jesus talking about matters of perspectives ever since his challenge to the rich man and then to Peter?

If perspective was Jesus' point, then, Jesus' culture of honor and shame would inform the interpretation of this strange tale. What the owner did, as the protesting workers rightly stated, was shameful. The owner, an unfair cheapskate, probably had quite a strange reputation if this was his normal way of operating his business. At the very worst, no one could understand him and in some sense, his reputation would have been questionable. Certainly, those who worked at the earliest shift probably would not want to work for him any more. They would then spread the bad word about him. If his reputation for this strange sense of generosity traveled to other workers, he would have trouble finding workers for the next day. His puzzling and eccentric personality would turn him off from many potential workers. But isn't this the point? The kingdom the Jesus taught was a very strange and eccentric institution. Its puzzling and checkered reputation would prevent many from participating in it, especially after observing the "generosity" of such a kingdom. No wonder many of Jesus' opponents continued to oppose him throughout Matthew. Social convention and human habits breed contempt. Sometimes, what was dishonorable in Jesus' society was honorable in the kingdom. This explains why so many still refused Jesus' offer. Whatever seemed like a good deal might not be a good deal, and whatever seemed like a bad deal could be a good deal.

At this point, we should summarize the present finding from the text itself. Jesus certainly pointed out that Peter did not give up that much in comparison to the return. The interpretation of kingdom investment is a matter of vision or perspectives. Jesus also pointed out that giving up for the kingdom was like being called from an impoverished state. The disciples should not sit around counting whether the call for work and sacrifice was fair because clearly without the call, they would be homeless and impoverished. To climax this series of discussions, Jesus talked about his sacrifice only to be misunderstood by the mother of Zebedee's sons. Jesus' followers still were talking about reward when Jesus was insisting on the kingdom value of sacrifice and the privilege of the call. When God is in charge (i.e., kingdom of heaven), his people will see God's generosity instead of their sacrifice. They will see all sacrifices as investment. Most people focus too much on the profound theological idea behind "first shall be last and last shall be first." Jesus seems to be saying something simple in 19:30 and 20:16: kingdom values turn worldly order upside down and his disciples had better get used to this upside down world.

PUTTING THE TEXT IN HISTORY:
MEANINGS FOR THE WORLD OF AUTHOR-READERS

Matthew's time was chaotic. While Peter gave up much in following Jesus, many also gave up their comfort in their society. With so many different groups being expelled from synagogues, they had to lose quite a lot. The question that arose would be, "What is in it for me?" Matthew's answer indicates that a lot would be in store for them in the future. Presently, Jesus taught that a new fictive family was part of the reward for his followers (19:29). These new groups were to live in the new identity. What kind of community would they be? They would live out the corporate personality of being the household of God.

In Matthew's time, relationships were means of transaction. In a patron-client society, the patron held all the power, but the client would receive fair treatment ideally. Relationships became a tug of war of give and take. The parable had eliminated any kind of transaction and absolutized the lordship of the owner. The kingdom of God was about the impossibility of measuring the divine call against the human idea of fairness, while rising above the system of the first-century society. Fairness presupposes that both sides have something the other side wants. Fairness could be part of the equation because citizens had nothing to offer God originally when they were standing around. Many might feel that they had offered so much already. The answer was that they really had nothing to offer. Without the call, they could do and earn nothing. While God appeared to reward, none of the reward could be earned by sacrifice because without Jesus' ultimate sacrifice, his followers were still lost and impoverished.

Jesus' sacrifice in 20:17–19 should mean something for Matthew's audience. Matthew was saying clearly that Jesus first paid the price that enabled the call to work in the kingdom. That price was larger than any price the disciples would imagine of paying themselves. As such, Christ-followers had no right to claim that they were not paid enough from the work in the farm.

How can we contextualize what has been said by Jesus in Matthew? Reward is inherently a human desire for the good works performed. There is a Chinese proverb that says, "Good will be rewarded with the good and evil for evil." Another western proverb is closer to the spirit of Peter, "Reward sweetens the labor." The fact of the matter is, reward cannot be the sole or even the primary motivation for giving up everything. Jesus showed clearly that the very fact someone could get anything from the kingdom, like those who were called to the agricultural work of the parable, was due to grace. In modern terms, the very fact one can give anything away for the kingdom came from the initial call of the kingdom. The call was and is unconditional. Grace allows one to work in the kingdom. Without that work and the grace of the call, every other person is much like those who stood around in Jesus' parable, never having any wages and possibly suffering a fate of starvation by poverty. Jesus was showing at once the richness of the call and the poverty of those who were called. Right at the center of that call was the complete sovereignty of God. Nothing could earn that call. No good work would measure up to the initial free grace.

In our society, we tend to think of fairness in terms of what one has earned. The parable dismissed fairness as something within human understanding and put both Jesus' own lordship and the richness of the call at the center of the parable. Matthew's Jesus did not end his teaching to Peter on reward. He climaxed with this parable to show the real focal point of the kingdom: God owes no one. By talking about the call in terms of the vineyard, he had relegated Peter's reward paradigm to a secondary place, while turning societal value, order, and fairness upside down. Peter thought his sacrifice was immense, but Jesus reminded him that the reward was greater. The trouble was that Peter did not realize that he had nothing to offer, evident in Peter thinking that his sacrifice would bring the comparable reward. Jesus reminded Peter that reward was never earned. The kingdom was not a bartering exercise like the transaction of patron-client society of Jesus and Matthew.

Christians these days can take a lesson from these stories. Many modern Peters still dabble in spiritual accounting that is not unlike the patron-client paradigm of the first century, instead of focusing on the preciousness of the kingdom or divine generosity towards all (20:15). What they give is nothing compared to what God has given. Somehow, after having believed for a while, many think that they have given so much to God and somehow God should "fairly" reward them. This is a real problem because some believers assume (wrongly) that somehow they are qualified to talk about reward and fairness with God. With God, no one is qualified to be his transaction partner. A believer who thinks "God is so lucky to have me because I give so much" should think "God has been so gracious in calling me in the first place. I should be willing to give all to the poor and follow Jesus." Relationship with God is not a transaction. Only through a true paradigm shift from transaction to gratitude will the believer begin to live out a proper understanding of these stories. Those who still bargain for reward hardly understand the preciousness of their call.

The parable can also be interpreted as a social perspective Jesus brought. Jesus analogized the kingdom to an oppressive system with many underprivileged employees. With little doubt, Jesus wanted Peter to identify himself with those employees who were desperate for work. Indirectly, the church should identify herself with the underprivileged, never taking for granted its resources as something deserved but something that came sole from a gracious God.

As my readers will notice, my backward telling of the story dissolves all tension and creates a picture of fairness. Fairness was expected by normal first-century practices. The owner did not only seem unfair. He seemed like a cheapskate who tried to hire as few people to work as possible and eventually found that he did not have enough. The normal owner would have had sense to hire enough workers to prevent shortage. Almost none of the way Jesus told was within the expectations of his audience. In the same way, God's kingdom was also quite unexpected, often surpassing the convention of his own people and sometimes varying quite far from the human scale of morality. As we have also seen above, "fairness" was never part of the formula for God's call. Neither was grace completely fair in human terms.

When preaching such a passage, preachers should take care not to dissolve the tension Jesus created. Here are some suggestions. Take care to emphasize that tension. Telling the story backwards is one way, and then keep on saying, "But the landowner is not doing what we expect." The constant theme should be "the kingdom is not what we expect." The structure of the sermon can easily become a kind of "surprise ending" when we draw in Peter's conversation with Jesus in comparison to Jesus' negation of Peter's concern for reward. The sermon format then can use most of the time to create that tension and then end up talking about Peter's concern at the last ten percent of the sermon. The surprising element should not be lost in any presentation because of Jesus' powerful rhetoric. In terms of application, the preacher can probably talk about the "this for that" mentality of our society, and then point the direction towards a bigger kingdom value: God is generous and gracious. Grace cannot be earned, and the kingdom does not always work out in the way we expect.

A preaching outline can look something like this, in accordance to the rhetorical force of Jesus' parable in Matthew.

Title: When fairness is not enough

Telling It Backward: the landowner is completely fair, giving each person his dues . . . but the kingdom is not like that. Do we serve a fair God?

1) What the world expects: reward for sacrifice
2) What Peter expects: reward for sacrifice
3) What the kingdom teaches: grace, generosity, God's rule, and Jesus' sacrifice

Conclusion: When grace comes into the picture, it is always trumps fairness. Whether God is fair is not the real issue.

REFLECTION QUESTIONS

1.   What is the tension expressed in the parable?

2.   How does the idea of fairness relate to the call of the landowner?

3.   What does the evil eye in 20:15 have to do with the entire context?

4.   Based on the entire context, is "reward" wrong?

5.   What parallel do you see in Christian practice today that violates the kingdom principles here?

6.   How are the values of Jesus different from his world's?

7.   How are these values different from our world's?

8.   How should the Christian live based on the "unfairness" paradigm in the parable?

9

Better Late than Never?

TELLING IT BACKWARD: MATTHEW 21:28-31

> Jesus told them this parable, "What do you think? A man had two
> sons. He went to the first and said, 'Son, go and work in the vine-
> yard today.' The boy answered, 'I will not.' The father went to the
> other son and said the same thing. This boy answered, 'I will, sir,'
> and went. Which of the two did his father's will?" They said, "The
> first." Jesus said to them, "I tell you the truth, tax collectors and
> prostitutes will go behind you into the kingdom of God! For John
> came to you in the way of righteousness, and you believed him.
> But the tax collectors and prostitutes did not believe."

A PATIENT WENT TO visit a doctor and said, "It has been a month since I
last visited, and I feel horrible." The doctor answered, "Did you follow the
directions?" The patient answered, "Sure did. The bottle said to keep the lid
tightly closed." When someone does not understand directions, all sorts of
miscues can happen. If the patient had understood and followed the directions, the illness might have gone away. However, sometimes patients have
the right directions in front of them, and still do not follow them. That is
when illnesses go from bad to worse.

Jesus' story has assumptions. It assumes that both sons already had
worked in the vineyard in the past. They were already instructed to do
this work. They knew what to do, and understood the meaning. They were
not told to navigate blindly without any understanding of how a vineyard

worked. I told the story backwards because under normal circumstances, having directions and understanding their meaning, the two sons ought to have stayed true to their words. The issue in this backward storytelling comes down to simple willingness. The one who said he would not do work continued in his laziness. The one who said he would went on to do the work. The first one represents the sinners Jesus named who continued to live in their sin, making them the worst in the kingdom. The chief priests and elders however taught the word and obeyed. So, they became the most important people of the kingdom. Yet, Jesus did not tell the story this way. Is saying "I will not do it" even a good option? We will think this through, along with other issues, in our discussion below.

TELLING IT NORMAL: KEY ELEMENTS IN THE STORY

> 28 "What do you think? A man had two sons. He went to the first and said, 'Son, go and work in the vineyard today.' 29 The boy answered, 'I will not.' But later he had a change of heart and went. 30 The father went to the other son and said the same thing. This boy answered, 'I will, sir,' but did not go. 31 Which of the two did his father's will?" They said, "The first." Jesus said to them, "I tell you the truth, tax collectors and prostitutes will go ahead of you into the kingdom of God! 32 For John came to you in the way of righteousness, and you did not believe him. But the tax collectors and prostitutes did believe. Although you saw this, you did not later change your minds and believe him.

I love watching little kids' martial arts classes because most of the time, they have no idea what they are doing, but they sure are enthusiastic about it. Whenever the teacher tells them to do something, inevitably the kids yell, "Yes, sir," sometimes followed by a little voice saying, "Can I go to the bathroom?" As they get older, the students begin to ask questions, and the "yes, sir" looks more like formality than enthusiasm. Sometimes, absolute obedience does not come immediately. Occasionally, the instructor must correct the older kid and say, "Not like that! You're making up your own style." Clearly, some just pay lip service to the "yes, sir." Jesus here shows the two kinds of people in the parable, the kind that obeys and the kind that does not.

What is better? That was the question Jesus put to his listeners. In order to understand this question, the narrative surrounding this story deserves a look. The origin of this story comes from Jesus' entrance to the temple court in 21:23. Before this entrance came a curse against the fruitless fig tree that symbolized the temple. Jesus cursed the tree, symbolic of the curse on the temple institution (21:18–22). The complicated explanation of the withered tree is outside the scope of the present discussion. All we need to know is Jesus' curse against the temple. Jesus was not unusual in his strong negative feelings against the temple, as the discussion about the usefulness of the temple was very much controversial in the period of Second Temple Judaism, and not all opinions were positive. Jesus was not the first to denounce the temple, and none of his denouncement came from anti-Semitism but from a debate about true religion.

The focal event that brought Jesus' parable came from 21:23–27. In Jesus' return to the temple court, top religious leaders questioned what authority Jesus had to do "these things." With a straightforward contextual reading, "these things" must include the destructive miracle against the fig tree, an act pregnant with social-political-theological meaning. When we view their question, we must note that they had seen "these things." It was not for the want of evidence they questioned Jesus. They presupposed "these things" were real. The dialogue that follows in 21:24–26 contains Jesus' challenging question to them, not so much to elicit an answer but to silence them. By recording the dialogue, Matthew demonstrated the true intentions of these religious leaders. They did not really want to know where Jesus' authority came from. They merely wanted to silence Jesus by throwing doubts around his listeners. Instead, Jesus silenced them by having the last word. This last word came form a pair of parables in 21:28–41, both of which mocked these religious leaders (21:45).

Jesus started with the story of the two sons in 21:28–30, followed by an explanation in 21:31–32, speaking of two sons having the ability and know-how to labor in the field. [1] The word Jesus used was "boys" in 21:28 to describe the sons. In 21:28, the term was used to describe the sons' biological and legal link with the father (cf. Mark 7:27ff; 10:29). [2] We must be careful not to read into the text our own modern convention of teen

---

1. There are actually three textual variations in the ancient manuscripts of the passage: 1) the first son said no but eventually repented and obeyed; 2) same as the first except with Jewish leaders stating that the second son was the obedient son; 3) the first son said yes but eventually did not obey. The three possible traditions not only represent variants but also ways the story could be interpreted.

2. No wonder this word "child" or "boy" is also used as a term of endearment in some of Jesus' conversations (e.g., Mark 10:24).

freedom to put aside their duties because the word here does not have an emphasis on age. In Jesus' day, children were under the complete authority of their parents. In the Roman household, these children had an obligation to honor the head of the household who, in this case, would be the father and vineyard owner. The very fact that the father gave the option showed a great deal of leniency even in an authoritative legal context. Jesus' usage of the word for "boys" shows the complete and utter absurdity of disobedience in an honor and shame society governed by certain legal codes. By telling the parable in this way, Jesus dismissed any legal reason for the boys to disobey. The usage further speaks of the dishonor of disobeying a biological parent, a crime of severe punishment in Jewish culture.

We can be sure that Jesus was not talking about little children, as Matthew had other vocabulary for younger children (e.g., Matt 18:2ff). Rather, Jesus was talking about the sons in terms of their legal and biological relationship with the father that obligated them to serve the father on the farm. One son said that he would not go work for the father but eventually changed his mind and worked. The other said he would, but never did. Jesus made a comparison between the two sons and asked which son was better. The religious leaders pointed to the first one. Matthew included their answer because their answer would condemn them when Jesus explained the parable.

The dialogue is also something that must be read in light of Jesus' society. When someone was honorable, he would let his positive confession match his positive action. The first son who had negative confession but positive action also did not fit the societal ideal, but at least positive action resulted. The second son had a positive confession without positive action. Thus, actions spoke louder than words for Jesus' audience.

Jesus explained the two sons in the parable as two types of people in the logical order of the story. First, Jesus talked about those tax collectors and prostitutes entering the kingdom. Jesus did not however say explicitly that they obeyed. He had skipped a logical step of saying that this group had done what God had told them. After all, these sinners were less knowledgeable than the religious leaders. As a result, the sinners took priority in the kingdom. Their original confession, much like the first son, was not even positive as an honor and shame society demanded, but at the very least, under less ideal conditions, positive action resulted.[3]

---

3. The honor-and-shame society requires its member to behave a certain way to gain approval. Positive confession to a higher power is such an honorable behavior.

Some modern readers would be confused about whether Jesus was talking about the religious leaders' eventual entrance to heaven. Jesus was not talking about going to heaven. Instead, he was talking about priority in the kingdom. The second explanation would clarify Jesus' point. Second, Jesus talked about the unbelief of the religious leaders versus the faith of the sinners in 21:32 (translated by the NIV as "repent"). Like the temple Jesus condemned, the religious leaders confessed all the right words, but failed in their action the same way the second son did. Here, Jesus referenced John the Baptist who was already mentioned in 21:24–27. If they did not believe John, the sinners who believed John (and Jesus) would usurp their place in the kingdom.

Jesus made a little more logical leap in his conclusion in 21:32 as well. If we were to match the parable with the characters in Jesus' audience (i.e., religious leaders, tax collectors, and prostitutes), then there was never a time when the religious leaders actually obeyed John verbally or practically. What leap did Jesus make that caused this parable to be interesting? Jesus at least had the disobedient son saying yes first. Most likely, Jesus was saying that the religious leaders never even said yes to God in words or deeds, while the tax collectors and prostitutes said no to God but obeyed God (in Jesus' teachings?). In Matthew's narrative, the religious leaders were even worse than the son who said yes and did nothing.

I retold the parable above in a backward fashion precisely because of the expectation people had of these religious leaders. The two sons did not have equal understanding of God's law! The less knowledgeable ended up obeying. Although the crowd could be double-minded, these leaders had far more qualifications to obey. They were the "good guys." Both in status and knowledge, they possessed clear advantage over sinners. As far as work was concerned, the labor was not too heavy but was all part of the duty for the boys in a family. Under normal circumstances, they would obey based on their knowledge and their status as minors under the rule of the father. The sinners who knowingly or unknowingly disobeyed would certainly not be above them but very much under them. Jesus reversed the norm. The radicalness of Jesus' parable comes from his calling them both "sons," even though the sinners had less knowledge about God's law. For Jesus' audience, this parable would have been a shocker. The parable is only half-finished as Jesus extended the vineyard story into the next parable before giving his conclusion. We shall discuss the next parable in the next chapter.

At the end of this discussion, obedience was not the only issue. In fact, obedience might not even be the main issue Jesus was addressing. Jesus was using obedience to talk about something else. What is that something else? The majority of the discussion that led to this parable had to do with authority. Jesus linked obedience to authority as a response to their inquiry about his authority. In other words, obedience is directly related to whether one recognizes that Jesus was the authority or not. The real issue is authority! The second son did not take the authority of the father seriously enough to do anything about obedience. The religious leaders (and the temple associated with them), throughout Matthew, had never explicitly promised that they would obey anything God or Jesus had to say to them, not for the lack of instruction or understanding but for the outright rejection of Jesus' authority. Jesus' condemnation was certainly when he used "change your minds/hearts" in 21:32, a verb already descriptive of the second son in 21:29. They were not the second son! Nor were they even the first son. When God is in charge (i.e., kingdom of heaven), the separation at the judgment centers on the question Jesus had posed before Peter, "Who do people say the Son of Man is?" (16:13)

PUTTING THE TEXT IN HISTORY: MEANINGS FOR THE WORLD OF AUTHOR-READERS

The parable is particularly painful for Matthew's audience. In the post-70 CE era, the Romans first threw them out of their religious comfort zone by the destruction of the temple. Furthermore, their compatriots who did not believe Jesus as the messiah threw them out of their comfortable religious community. This double-alienation created difficulties for Matthew's audience. The problem of course had to do with their agitators not recognizing Jesus' authority. Moreover, these same agitators not only held important positions in their synagogue and society, but also held superior knowledge of the Torah. At least, their knowledge was the public perception. Equally difficult would be the religious life of Matthew's community. We have to remember that the synagogue possessed all the Scriptures. Separation would be very inconvenient, even from a practical sense. How could they worship or practice their faith without their Scriptures? The synagogue authorities had no obligation to release those copies to be copied.

The parable presented a sharper edge for Matthew's audience as well because it talked favorably about tax collectors who worked for the Romans, the same enemies who destroyed the temple, by profiting from the fees the Romans paid for them collecting from their own people. Essentially, the tax collectors were traitors. Here Jesus said that those who obeyed the Father happened to be the traitors to the physical kingdom of Israel while those who looked respectable in the kingdom were actually the cursed. Those respectable religious people were worse than traitors. By using this kind of rhetoric, the parable basically created a command for Matthew's community to make a clear separation from those disobedient but apparently respectable members of Israel.

Matthew's solution to such a situation was to present Jesus as the authoritative teacher who deserved obedience. Whether Matthew's solution was too simplistic, he provided a way out. Matthew basically said through the parable that obedience to Israel's God, the prime owner of the vineyard, was to listen to Jesus. In order to listen, the community member had to recognize Jesus as authoritative first.

Christianity today has evolved into such a shape that the faith community is defined more by its doctrinal stance (e.g., Calvinists/Reformed, Lutheran, etc.) than by its praxis (e.g., Baptists). Even non-denominational churches define themselves by a text (i.e., "Bible" churches) they promise to study. Judaism was and in a certain degree still is defined very much by its praxis (e.g., keeping Sabbath, kosher food, circumcision, worship of YHWH). Jesus' parable applied in Matthew's community also steered towards praxis. The identity of the group was not only about accepting but also about practicing Jesus' teaching. Even traitors to the Romans could practice Jesus' teachings. So could morally questionable prostitutes. How much more should Matthew's community walk in Jesus' way?

With the corporate personality of Matthew's community being built on praxis, the true expression of the community was not merely in what it preached or claimed but also in its witness. In the same way, in modern living, faith is known less for its belief (e.g., "I believe in the Trinity.") as much as for its practice (e.g., "We don't have sex before we get married."). In some ways, the outsider knows the faith community's "belief" from its praxis. Matthew's emphasis on obedience to the authority of Jesus still rings true today. Besides knowing that Christians believe in Jesus, most people do not learn Christianity from doctrine. The more non-Christian the society is, the less the society will know about Christian doctrine. Quite often, the praxis of the faith community can lead to more misunderstanding (e.g., "All Christians are anti-gay and anti-sex.") than understanding.

Matthew's community faced the challenge of not so much what its community believed but how its community might reach "all people." In other words, after Matthew's community had to face a non-Jewish society, its posture was extremely important. The same goes for the faith community in the twenty-first century. In western society, the mission field is not "out there" but "among us." Like the backward telling of my story, those who know more should be able to obey even more. The problem today, with the information explosion, is that knowledge is never the problem. Praxis is. This passage is not so hard to preach. The preacher can utilize a format that originally talks about the parable before concluding that the real issue is not obedience but authority. The outline can look something like this.

Title: Better Late than Never?
Telling It Backward: Those who know better would do better . . .
but the kingdom is not like that. Would knowledge help obedience?

1) Late (21:28–29)
2) Never (21:30)
3) Explanation (21:31–32): those who should know better do nothing.
4) Real Issue (21:23)
Conclusion: the real issue is not knowledge but authority. Who is our authority?

REFLECTION QUESTIONS

1. What assumptions did Jesus make when telling the story of the two sons?

2. Why does seeing the two sons as minors make a difference?

3. What logical leap did the story make and why?

4. How does telling the story backward dissolve the tension?

5. What was the real issue besides obedience?

6. How was the real issue related to obedience?

10

When Patience Runs Out

TELLING IT BACKWARD: MATTHEW 21:33-46

> Jesus said: "Listen to another parable: There was a landowner who planted a vineyard. He put a fence around it, dug a pit for its winepress, and built a watchtower. Then he leased it to tenant farmers and went on a journey. When the harvest time was near, he sent his slaves to the tenants to collect his portion of the crop. The tenants welcomed the slaves and gave an account, and the owner rewarded the tenants for their faithful service."

PREACHERS WHO RESEARCH ON the internet will discover that most discussions about stewardship are in monetary terms. It seems that people see stewardship purely from the perspective of money. The same perspective also applied in Jesus' day. Therefore, Jesus told a story about money invested in a vineyard. Under normal circumstances, the landowner would be in a winning situation. He did not become a landowner by squandering his inheritance. He would invest wisely and hire competent workers to ensure a profit would come. This story develops under normal circumstances where profit was the end result. Yet, neither Jesus nor Matthew told the story in this backward fashion.

TELLING IT NORMAL: KEY ELEMENTS IN THE STORY

33 "Listen to another parable: There was a landowner who planted a vineyard. He put a fence around it, dug a pit for its winepress, and built a watchtower. Then he leased it to tenant farmers and went on a journey. 34 When the harvest time was near, he sent his slaves to the tenants to collect his portion of the crop. 35 But the tenants seized his slaves, beat one, killed another, and stoned another. 36 Again he sent other slaves, more than the first, and they treated them the same way. 37 Finally he sent his son to them, saying, 'They will respect my son.' 38 But when the tenants saw the son, they said to themselves, 'This is the heir. Come, let's kill him and get his inheritance!' 39 So they seized him, threw him out of the vineyard, and killed him. 40 Now when the owner of the vineyard comes, what will he do to those tenants?" 41 They said to him, "He will utterly destroy those evil men! Then he will lease the vineyard to other tenants who will give him his portion at the harvest."

42 Jesus said to them, "Have you never read in the scriptures: 'The stone the builders rejected has become the cornerstone. This is from the Lord, and it is marvelous in our eyes'?

43 For this reason I tell you that the kingdom of God will be taken from you and given to a people who will produce its fruit. 44 The one who falls on this stone will be broken to pieces, and the one on whom it falls will be crushed." 45 When the chief priests and the Pharisees heard his parables, they realized that he was speaking about them. 46 They wanted to arrest him, but they were afraid of the crowds, because the crowds regarded him as a prophet.

In the corporate world, bosses often give employees performance evaluations. I have seen some funny ones: "Since my last evaluation, this employee has reached rock bottom. Now he's starting to dig." "The employee has a delusion of adequacy." "He sets low standards, but fails even at those." "The challenge of deadline is only made more difficult by having this employee on the team."

I suppose all employers are looking for employees who work faster than a speeding bullet, rather than ones who shoot themselves in the foot, but most are just satisfied with a good profit and loyalty. In Jesus' story, the employees have reached a new low. Such negative results would have dire consequences.

This parable in 21:33–41 is a continuation of 21:28–32. In fact, it acts as the climax of Jesus' response to the challenge against his authority. This climax also includes the next parable in 22:1–14. However, 22:1–14 will be the topic of the next chapter. For now, let us focus on 21:33–41.

The start of this story is in 21:23 where the religious authorities challenged Jesus' authority for doing "these things." We have discussed their real challenge in the last chapter. This parable then, just like the parable of the two sons in 21:28–32, acted as Jesus' condemnation of their challenge. The parable's plot goes something like this.

The landowner had planted the vineyard and hired people so that he could reap a great harvest in 21:33–34. These tenant farmers would work for the owner with their skills in exchange for living accommodation and part of the harvest. Although the tenant farmers were not wealthy, they had enough skills to be entrepreneurs who could produce something for the absentee owner. Although some scholars see the system of owner-tenant farmers as oppressive, Jesus seems to assume that the owner deserved his part of the pay. At least, under normal circumstances, they would respect the owner's terms and pay the owner his dues while pulling in some profit. However, this circumstance was anything but normal. Instead of paying the owner's share to the collectors who were the owner's slaves, the tenants committed increasing violence against the collectors, even causing death in 21:35. As the owner continued to send collectors, the level of violence also increased. Finally, the owner thought that sending his son would solve the problem. After all, in the honor and shame society of Israel, people would not dare to commit such dishonor against the son. At this point, Matthew readers must have appreciated the great patience of the owner. It would not have been normal even for Matthew's time that the owner would exercise this kind of patience because Jesus' conclusion showed his audience that the owner was well capable of killing these violent criminals. Jesus questioned his listeners on the right course of action against these criminals in 21:41.

Contrary to the popular image of a loving sage, Jesus did not disagree with the listeners' assessment that the tenants deserved a violent death by the militiamen the owner hired to collect his share. The audience answered that the owner not only ought to kill the bad farmers, but should also hire other responsible and honorable farmers. The audience knew the conclusion because that would have been what happened in Jesus' day. There were only two shockers in the story: the degree of dishonor the tenant farmers possessed and the owner's hesitance to use swift justice to collect his money.

The above story indicates two facts. First, the owner could have immediately hired other farmers to till his vineyard. These bad tenant farmers were not the only people who had skills. Second, the owner's patience went beyond the norm. Jesus now explained the parable. Jesus used Ps 118:22–23 as the scriptural explanation. As usual, both the audiences of Jesus and of Matthew knew this Psalm because they would regularly sing it in synagogue worship. The Psalm is full of interesting insights to illuminate the present situation.

First, the responsive portion of the Psalm (118:1–4) has "His love endures forever." This portion points directly to the patience of the vineyard owner. Moreover, for those returning from exile, the "builders" of Israel point to Israel's leaders during the return from exile. Who else should be expected to rebuild the temple and Israel? However, those "builders" had indeed rejected the owner and the son. The next portion of the Psalm (118:5–12) talks of the attack of the enemies, presumably the gentile nations (118:10), but God would destroy them at the end. This portion points directly to the vengeful finale of the parable. A most ironic analogy of this part is that the nations, not true people of God, were attacking the Psalmist. In the story Matthew told, the religious authorities and not the nations were attacking Jesus. The portion leading up to Jesus' quotation proclaims the good ending and thanksgiving of the righteous (118:13–21). Thus, the ultimate conclusion of the story, as Jesus used the quotation, would be a positive one.

Jesus' quotation of Ps 118:22–23 is an analogy of the triumph of the rejected and oppressed, much like a useless piece of building material with original importance that had been discarded. This material would be restored to its rightful place when God interceded. Jesus then provided the explanation of his assessment of Ps 118:22–23. The stone would serve to cause damage either by becoming a stumbling block or by being a weapon of mass destruction.

When looking at the story, many interpreters want to identify the exact meaning of the vineyard. Snodgrass sees the vineyard as God's work instead of Israel.[1] Perhaps it is ultimately best to see God's work IN Israel instead of choosing the vineyard as either God's work or Israel. As God moved the work away from Israel, the work originally in Israel (i.e. temple leadership) would be given to someone else (i.e. quite possibly the early apostolic leaders). The vineyard parable here is obviously and logically related to the previous parable because both have a setting of vineyard. In the previous parable, the two sons analogized the two kinds of people. The two kinds were those who had high religious standing but would not obey

---

1. Snodgrass, *Stories with Intent*, 274.

and those who had the lowest religious standing but obeyed. Logically, the shorter story of the two sons serves as the introduction for the more elaborate story here about the tenant farmers. The story of the two sons categorized the people into two kinds with the second kind being the bad ones. The emphasis of the first story is the lack of action.

The second story, the tenant farmer story, continues where the first story left off. Jesus showed that the second son (or the kind people represented by him) was not completely inactive. Instead, he was full of bad action that produced nothing the kingdom demanded, as evidenced by what the bad tenant farmers did in the vineyard. Instead of productive work, they used their time to formulate their scheme to take over the harvest and the land. Upon taking over the vineyard, they attacked those who came to the vineyard to serve the master. Finally, this bad lot would lose their place through death and the vineyard would be handed over to those who would serve faithfully. Popular interpreters might see the gentiles as those who would take over the vineyard but immediate context demands us to see them as the seemingly irreligious tax collectors and prostitutes (21:32). Little wonder the religious leaders wanted to arrest Jesus because Jesus had turned their world upside down with this combination of two parables about the vineyard. What an outrage! What an insult!

The moral of the pair of parables then is simple. Jesus asserted several truths about the kingdom. First, the knowledge of the religious leaders did not save them. Instead, their knowledge condemned them. They knew how to till the vineyard but disobeyed the owner. They had forfeited their position in the kingdom. Second, religious standing was secondary compared to the willingness to work. Many interpreters would go further to see the vineyard as Israel, drawing upon Old Testament symbolism (e.g., Isa 5:1–7). This understanding is probably correct, especially when these leaders were in charge of Israel. Third, the evil tenant farmers typified all the evil leaders of Israel's past because the story had many different servants going to the vineyard until the son came. Some suggest that the many servants in the parables were prophets who served God faithfully but met persecution for their hard work. Essentially, Jesus indicted the religious leaders with Israel's historic sins. No wonder the leaders wanted to arrest Jesus.

Jesus had concluded his story with a violent ending in 21:41, similar to 13:42, 50, 22:13, and 24:51. Such endings have one thing in common. They serve to condemn. We may not like Jesus' intolerant language in our society, but we cannot avoid the conclusion that Jesus' violent language conveys the gravest consequence for those who rejected his authority.

PUTTING THE TEXT IN HISTORY:
MEANINGS FOR THE WORLD OF AUTHOR-READERS

The experience of Matthew's community in this world would cause them to think about how to express the kingdom. Their rejection from some of their kinsmen would further put them at a disadvantage. The story serves as a comforting thought for the alienated community. Those who condemned Matthew's community would be condemned themselves. At the same time, it opens up possibility for new mission.

In 21:43, the others who would be included in the kingdom were not any of the religious leaders, especially not those who rejected Matthew and his community. Instead, those who were formerly considered sinners would receive their place in the kingdom. Matthew's community then would seek out sinners and even gentiles instead of focusing on only reaching Jews. Every rejection became an opportunity for inclusion of the formerly excluded people groups.

It is easy to read monetary terms into the parable because it contains monetary issues in its plot. We must pay attention to the fact that parables act like metaphors, using one theme to talk about another message. This parable teaches a fantastic lesson to the modern human. It teaches that stewardship should not merely address monetary issues. Rather, stewardship is ultimately about the authority of Jesus. What we do with Jesus' authority directly dictates what we do with life. Since Jesus was dealing with his authority when he answered the question by this parable, we must see ourselves as the stewards of Jesus' authority. Matthew had handed down a message about Jesus' authority to the modern reader. The faith community must take care to respond properly to that authority and become a good steward of this message. In this message, not respecting Jesus' authority equals not being a good steward with all that Jesus had entrusted to the world. A neglectful steward will face dire consequences.

Matthew's story concretely challenges us to apply ourselves in the faith community today. I saw a church sign that says something like "God prefers kind atheists over hateful Christians." Clearly, we do not know whom God actually prefers. Who is to know the mind of God? I can however appreciate the frustration this sign expresses. Today, there are many in the faith community who are more like the first son. There are even those who are like the evil tenant farmers who took over the farm. Their ownership of the kingdom business causes them to ignore and dishonor Jesus' authority. With such religious leaders, the faith community no longer demonstrates the kingdom. Instead, other unexpected people would show it in other forms. We have to appreciate the fact that Jesus (or Matthew) was telling these controversial parables to the faith community and not to those outside of it (e.g., gentiles) where many chose to live the backward narrative.

The homiletic application of this text should be on the power the owner had, much like the power God has in judgment day. At the same time, the narrative has a balance in the owner's patience. This story is an analogy of what would eventually happen with the rejection of Jesus. One day, when God's patience runs out, bad things will happen. Bad things would have to happen towards God's salvation history before anything good comes out of it.

Title: When Patience Runs Out
Telling It Backward: In a society where tenant farmers depended on landowner's wealth, the workers would faithfully work . . .
but reality is very different. Does God prefer kind atheists to hateful Christians?

1) The Patience of the Owner Tested (21:35–36)
2) The Patience of the Owner Exhausted (21:37–39)
3) The Owner's Final Solution (21:40–46)
Conclusion: Sometimes, the problem is not the knowledge possessed by the tenant farmer. God prefers believers to respect his authority.

REFLECTION QUESTIONS

1. Is money the real issue? Why or why not?

2. How did Jesus construct the role of his authority in the parable?

3. Did the tenant farmers have enough knowledge about the way of farming and the honor system?

4. Who were some possible candidates for other tenant farmers in 21:43?

5. What does the parable say about "ownership" of a ministry?

6. Who was Jesus talking to, those outside or inside his faith community?

7. What are the implications for modern believers?

11

When Dishonor Reaches Its Limit

TELLING IT BACKWARD: MATTHEW 22:1–14

> Jesus spoke to them again in parables, saying: "The kingdom of heaven can be compared to a king who gave a wedding banquet for his son. When he sent his slaves to summon those who had been invited to the banquet, they all came. Everyone was excited. Some who were invited even extended hospitality to the king's slaves. Everyone was properly dressed and the banquet brought great rejoicing for both hosts and guests alike. Many who are called feel privileged to be part of this great kingdom event."

WHENEVER WE HEAR ABOUT a person's son or daughter getting married, our natural reaction is to congratulate them. We may not be best friends with such people, but the proper etiquette requires us to congratulate them. Jesus' society also had its own etiquette. The above story demonstrates normal etiquette in Jesus' society, but the passage of Matthew 22:1–14 is anything but normal. In a society that valued harmony and reciprocity, the host's generous gesture ought to be met with a loud cheer, followed by a scramble to buy gifts to honor the host and his son. Yet, neither Jesus nor Matthew told the story in this backward fashion.

TELLING IT NORMAL: KEY ELEMENTS IN THE STORY

> Jesus spoke to them again in parables, saying: 2 "The kingdom of heaven can be compared to a king who gave a wedding banquet for his son. 3 He sent his slaves to summon those who had been invited to the banquet, but they would not come. 4 Again he sent other slaves, saying, 'Tell those who have been invited, "Look! The feast I have prepared for you is ready. My oxen and fattened cattle have been slaughtered, and everything is ready. Come to the wedding banquet."' 5 But they were indifferent and went away, one to his farm, another to his business. 6 The rest seized his slaves, insolently mistreated them, and killed them. 7 The king was furious! He sent his soldiers, and they put those murderers to death and set their city on fire. 8 Then he said to his slaves, 'The wedding is ready, but the ones who had been invited were not worthy. 9 So go into the main streets and invite everyone you find to the wedding banquet.' 10 And those slaves went out into the streets and gathered all they found, both bad and good, and the wedding hall was filled with guests. 11 But when the king came in to see the wedding guests, he saw a man there who was not wearing wedding clothes. 12 And he said to him, 'Friend, how did you get in here without wedding clothes?' But he had nothing to say. 13 Then the king said to his attendants, 'Tie him up hand and foot and throw him into the outer darkness, where there will be weeping and gnashing of teeth!' 14 For many are called, but few are chosen."

In many Asian cultures, even today, wedding banquets are occasions for great show of power, reciprocity, and camaraderie. Such occasions maintain the complex relationships not just within the family but also among extended family, business associations, and general friendships. Sometimes, even business associates get invited. Quite often, those invited send representatives from their families if they themselves cannot make the occasion. Many have expectations of invitation for the weddings of colleagues' sons and daughters. In my own wedding, I had many guests whom I have never met and might never meet again. They are relatives of relatives or friends of the extended family who were invited by our families. Although this seems like a strange practice to my western friends, it is the norm in some Asian cultures. Ideally, such a complex structure provides a network and mutual support in social and business dealings. This kind of extended invitation seems to be a financial burden to the bride and groom today, as the budget often surpasses the resources of the young couple and their family. For my western friends, this practice would break the bank of the new couple because the gift giving habits in the West are quite different from many Asian societies (even in the Asian-American society). In the norm of many Asian societies, however, the guests would all bring cash to cover their own meals plus extra gift money to help the young couple establish their financial status. In the future, reciprocity is very much expected.

Ideally, many Asian societies use reciprocity to maintain social balance. All honorable hosts know what to do: to invite all those in their relational circle to their children's wedding banquet. All honorable guests know what to do also: to give monetary gifts large enough to cover both the cost of the meal and the cost of buying household items for the new couple. When a wedding occurs, the tradition of reciprocity must be honored. If people fail to honor this network and tradition, relationships may be broken, sometimes irreparably. My own ethnic culture has a lot of parallel with this parable, but this parable is so much more severe because the patron is not just some socially superior person but a king, a person of the highest social standing.

This parable continues Jesus' previous two parables in 21:28–46. Jesus was not finished because he was still in the same place, talking to the same people. The basis of such a parable came from the social networking of the Jewish world, much like the Asian example I have given above. We may notice the progressively worse situation through the entire story. In this way, this story is a hardening of the last story about the vineyard. Both stories progressively worsen. All these stories in 21:28—22:14 deal with Jesus' authority being questioned in 21:23–27.

First, in this story, the king invited people via his slaves in 22:3. The honorable answer in that society would be, "I'll come at all costs." Refusal would already dishonor the host. Yet, this dishonor only increased in Jesus' telling of the story. The king did not feel discouraged with the initial refusal but sent more invitations via his slaves in 22:4. The word for the meal "feast" could well mean something like a big meal starting around noon and running into the evening with guests trickling in. The slave would announce for the king all the benefits of this banquet including the good food and the readiness. Yet, such great benefits did not move anyone. Just when it seems impossible that dishonor could get worse, it does. Three different responses were given in 22:5. Some left, some went back to farming, and some went to do business, as if the king's invitation was never sent. Yet, the dishonor increased in Jesus' story. The rest of the people who did pay attention took the slaves, beat them, and killed them in 22:6. Reading this would certainly make even a modern reader angry. Imagine if you invite your acquaintances and all your acquaintances decide to ignore you, and those who actually paid attention beat up and kill the messenger? The king rightly became angry and used his kingly power to exact revenge.

The king then went out to invite those who normally would not step foot into the king's hall to eat with the king in 22:8–10. The phrase "both bad and good" also indicates that the king's invitation was now greatly inclusive. Yet, the story took one more strange twist. Someone came improperly dressed in 22:11. In ancient times, appropriate clothing signified appropriate identity in each occasion. This person obviously did not have an excuse, because when questioned he was speechless. The king then threw him out into the darkness. Matthew had given this kind of harsh ending in 13:42, 50, 22:13, and 24:51, showing this type of parable to be similar in kind to those passages. These types of parables point to an eschatological event where God will separate some for the messianic kingdom (in this case, banquet) and some for judgment. At the end, Jesus' conclusion consists of a proverbial saying about many being called but few elected.

Jesus' final saying deserves unpacking. Who were the many and who were the few in the parable? Clearly, the many were all those who were called. It seems that some had chosen to ignore the call. Those who ignored the call or, worse yet, actively did something against such a call (e.g., murder of the slaves) seem to be entirely making their personal choice. The ones elected included those who were not normally invited, even the "bad" people. These who accepted the call seem to be entirely making their personal choice also. However, Jesus said something different. Although people thought they were making their own choices, ultimately, God was the one making the choice. More importantly, God had chosen those who normally would not fit into his household. The last indeed became the first, not because God favored the last, but because the lazy son (21:28–32), the thuggish tenant farmers (21:33–44), and the criminal guests that refused the banquet invitation (22:1–7) repeatedly insulted God.

When we view the story in the greater scheme of the three parables, those who were chosen were the tax collectors and prostitutes in 21:31. Those who were rejected were the religious leaders. In the first parable in 21:28–32, Jesus clearly addressed the Pharisees. In the second parable in 21:33–46, the Pharisees certainly wore the shoes that fit in Jesus' condemnation (cf. 21:45). Finally, here, they definitely got the message much like the last parable because the Pharisees had chosen to go out to scheme against Jesus. In fact, their hatred was so great that they teamed up with the Herodians who served the Romans to attack Jesus. Former enemies (i.e., Pharisees and Herodians) would now gather under one banner to reject Christ, thus completing also their rejection by God. This parable also has a strongly prophetic feel before the eschatological discourse starting in Matthew 24. It also points toward the Passion of Jesus, an event with an eschatological indicator of what the enraged king would do.

The three parables from 21:28—22:13 also share roughly the same plotline, evident by the following comparative outlines.

Parable:	The call and responses:	The result:
Parable of the Sons	21:28–30	21:31–32
Parable of the Tenants	21:33–39	21:40–45
Parable of the Banquet	22:1–12	22:13

The three parables from 21:28—22:13 also give different emphases, based on the kind of stories they told. The first parable in 21:28–32 is a family parable, denoting the father-son relationship. Quite reasonably, in those days, sons should obey their fathers. This relationship of respect was the social norm. The second parable in 21:33–44 is a land ownership parable, denoting the great power and right the owner had over the land. Any kind of disrespect towards landowners would completely destroy the society. The third parable in 22:1–13 is a social parable, denoting social network that caused the society to function. The authority and provision of the king surely was greater than even the father or the landowner. The logic of these three parables goes from intimate to official, from household to society, and from great to greatest. If anyone upset the elements within the normal practice of any of the three stories, the end result would be social chaos. By noting the violations, Jesus covered from the smallest to the greatest offenses against the most intimate relationship to the most official, to show an utter disregard for order and authority from all the villains of these parables. The villains' total and absolute disruption of these boundaries finally would create irreparable chaos in the kingdom. They had to be dealt with or Israel's society would fall apart completely. Thus, the banquet was a strong call from Jesus for commitment. It was no casual affair, as the climactic expulsion of the improperly dressed man shows. The power of the king demanded commitment. This set of parables more than adequately prepared Jesus' audience for the call to be alert and take the kingdom seriously in the later eschatological discourse.

I told the parable backward to illustrate a point that comes from normal social interaction. Under good circumstances, people would respect the king. There was no reason to reject the king and actively make the king the enemy. After all, the king was powerful and could provide the kind of connection people needed. If people recognized the king's social status, they would not treat him in this way. To mistreat and kill the king's slave would be a direct attack on the king's good will. What kind of people would ignore a king's invitation? What kind of people would go a step further to abuse the ones sending invitations to the extent of killing them? These were idiotic people! At least Matthew's Jesus wanted us to believe that these people were supremely stupid and evil. Reading such a story would make a first-century person highly indignant with white-hot anger. Why would anyone not be angry listening to Jesus' story? Such was the rhetorical force of Jesus' parable. Jesus thus pronounced a powerful condemnation of his enemies.

One thing my readers may notice is my resistance to allegorize the parables as much as I can because these parables together weave together a greater picture that illustrates Jesus' kingdom principles rather than typological characters representing this or that group. The villains in Mathew would become apparent only when they violated the principles Jesus laid out.

PUTTING THE TEXT IN HISTORY: MEANINGS FOR THE WORLD OF AUTHOR-READERS

The banquet parable speaks volumes to Matthew's situation. The situation in Matthew's community demanded a certain reading of the wedding banquet parable. Matthew's community could have two possible kinds of membership. First, it could contain a majority of ritualistically pure and moral Jews. Their purity and morality marked their identity. So did their belief in Christ. Second, Matthew's community could also have a mixture of tax collectors and prostitutes. This mixture would create a problem because it would draw more of the same kind of people. In either situation, the faith community would be going through a very rough transition.

At the same time, Matthew's community would slowly but surely move out of the original synagogue situation where people rejected Jesus as the messiah. If the synagogue rejected Jesus, they would have to consider those who crucified Jesus to be right. Would Matthew's community consider those same people to be right? The wedding banquet parable strongly asserted that those who rejected Jesus' offer of God's kingdom would not be part of the banquet. In the worst case, they would be like those who killed other servants of God in salvation history. They faced condemnation. This parable encouraged Matthew's community to forego their comfort zone and break out from those who rejected Jesus as the messiah. The banquet parable surely focused on the identity (i.e., clothing of the last character) of each member. All people in the community ought to consider carefully their own identity. A person could not take on identities of both those who rejected and accepted Jesus as the true authority from God. To arrive at the banquet with the right clothing means to have a singular identity.

To be part of the king's banquet was indeed a huge privilege. Matthew's community would also be encouraged greatly by the parable, knowing that they had a place at the messianic banquet. In a patron-client setting, being part of the patron's household would allow one to have many privileges closed to outsiders. More importantly, 22:14 talks of God's choice of the believers. This choice put them at the privileged position, even though their worldly position was less desirable. The ending served to encourage Matthew's community to stay the course. At the same time, in exaggerated rhetoric, Matthew showed that rejection of Jesus was a ludicrous as rejecting a king's banquet.

Reflecting on Matthew's message for today's faith community, Jesus' parable makes a very basic point. Even though kingdom membership is diverse, its identity (i.e., clothing) is singular. The commonality has to be the acceptance of the banquet invitation with the singular focus of seeing Jesus as the messiah. Everything else comes second. This parable also challenges the modern faith community on whether their expression to the outsider can or will convey that same identity. Matthew's community would reach Jews and gentiles alike. Its posture toward the outside ought to express its identity. When the outside world encounters the modern faith community, I wonder what kind of image the community conveys.

A while back, there was a video called "Why I hate religion and love Jesus" on YouTube.[1] In it, the speaker talks about failures of religion in clever rhymes against the personal relationship with God Jesus brought. Whether we agree with that dichotomy between religion and personal relationship

---

1. http://www.youtube.com/watch?v=1IAhDGYlpqY, accessed March 22, 2013.

with God, the faith community creates institutionalized religion. The very fact this video went viral shows the world's perception of the faith community. Thus, the faith community has a PR problem. Jesus' parable uses the banquet to show the importance of being attached to the right patron, God himself, so that the mission to the world would convey the right message. For Matthew, there were two kinds of people in 22:14, the elect and non-elect. I wonder: when the world looks at the faith community today, does it see the community's own identity as the elect community?

The kingdom invitation was rejected many times in Jesus' parable. People went about their everyday living, being distracted by this or that. This is a great parable for our time as well, when people who ought to be kingdom citizens drift here and there in their status quo lives. Sooner or later, the faith community will lose its focus and identity in its own mediocrity. The kingdom however resists status quo but advocates change. If "religion" shows the singular identity of Jesus, then people would no longer need to "hate religion but love Jesus." Yet, Jesus represents change and not status quo. Jesus' challenge should also be part of our homiletical execution of this text.

The homiletic application of this parable could be rough and risky. We must be quite careful not to turn our rhetoric into anti-Semitism. Surely, those who rejected God's invitations were Jews, but so was Matthew's community. We must be careful not to denigrate Jews just because Matthew seems to be doing so. If Matthew's community received the invite and the other Jews did not, the focus was not on ethnicity but on the privilege of reception and identity of the attendee. The previous insults from those who rejected the invitation probably are not as relevant to today because they were specific to certain historical circumstances in Jesus' day. It would be unfair to bring up that situation because there are not many exact parallels today. The preacher simply cannot assume that the rejection of Jesus today is the same as the rejection of Jesus in first century. There are legitimate reasons why so many reject the faith today. Rejection happens quite often because of ignorance or bad PR of the church. I would even suggest a completely opposite perspective of seeing the benefits of the king rather than his wrath simply because rejection of the king was never a reasonable or believable option. My focus can be on the results rather than the problem because the problem would have been clear without any retelling. I would suggest a sermon that looks like the following.

Title: The King with Benefits

Telling It Backward: The king's invite is an honor, and people gladly come . . . but Jesus portrayed a different reality. How do people respond to the kingdom?

1) First Way to Forgo Benefits (22:1–7)
2) Second Way to Forgo Benefits (22:8–13)
Conclusion: God chooses to be a benefactor but sometimes people do not accept the benefits or their identity in the kingdom (22:14).

REFLECTION QUESTIONS

1. What is the logic behind the three parables in 21:28—22:14?

2. What are the emphases in the three parables?

3. What is so unusual about the wedding banquet parable?

4. Why is clothing a problem, based on first-century culture?

5. Why does the ending in 22:14 talks about God's choice rather than human choice?

12

Be Yourself? Know Your Place!

TELLING IT BACKWARD: MATTHEW 24:45-51

> Jesus asked, "Who then is the faithful and wise slave, whom the master has put in charge of his household, to give the other slaves their food at the proper time? Blessed is that slave whom the master finds at work when he comes. I tell you the truth, the master will put him in charge of all his possessions. If a good slave should say to himself, 'My master is staying away a long time but can show up any time,' and because he believes in his master's potential reward, he treats his fellow slaves well and keeps the estate free of riffraffs, then the master of that slave will come on the day and hour he is expected, and won't the slave receive the reward he deserves?"

HOW MANY HOURS DOES the average American actually work? This is not an easy question to answer. The estimate by some researchers comes to six per day or less. Some even estimate as little as two to three hours in an eight-hour day. A lot of the time, people browse the web for personal interests. Perhaps, without the computer and other electronic devices, people might actually work more. With the computer, their bosses can no longer catch them doing something else on company time because they have multiple windows opened while working. How this will impact American productivity in the long run remains uncertain, but most bosses would probably want to get more than two to six hours out of the employee's eight-hour workday. This story Jesus told certainly deals with productivity and serving the boss's interest.

In the way I told this story above, the slave was very much faithful to his task. In Jesus' society, a slave did not really have any legal freedom to be anything other than faithful. In some literature, slaves served as the owner's extension and tool of his ambition. In other words, an unfaithful slave was so much worse than the unfaithful employee of modern work force. Thus, my backward story above suggests the ancient ideal to be the norm. Yet, neither Jesus nor Matthew told the story in this backward fashion. Jesus told a story that did not fit the norm or the ideal.

TELLING IT NORMAL: KEY ELEMENTS IN THE STORY

> 45 "Who then is the faithful and wise slave, whom the master has put in charge of his household, to give the other slaves their food at the proper time? 46 Blessed is that slave whom the master finds at work when he comes. 47 I tell you the truth, the master will put him in charge of all his possessions. 48 But if that evil slave should say to himself, 'My master is staying away a long time,' 49 and he begins to beat his fellow slaves and to eat and drink with drunkards, 50 then the master of that slave will come on a day when he does not expect him and at an hour he does not foresee, 51 and will cut him in two, and assign him a place with the hypocrites, where there will be weeping and gnashing of teeth."

Some of the best lines I hear come from excuses of people being caught slacking (or even in some cases, sleeping) at work. Here are some I see on the internet joke websites. "I'm working smarter, not harder." "I'm meditating on the company mission statement." "The blood bank told me that this would happen." "Someone must have put the decaf in the wrong pot." For the best response, (I actually heard this one) one person said to the boss, "I thought you were gone for the day." These may be hilarious excuses, but they probably would not amuse the boss very much. However, the unfaithful slave in Jesus' parable here moves one step beyond slacking.

This parable is part of an illustration for Jesus' saying in 24:42–44. It is a private teaching Jesus gave exclusively to his disciples (24:1–3). The disciples' focus was "when" while Jesus' focus was something else. Jesus was adamant about the need to be alert. Such an illustrative parable extends to 25:1–46. All these parables have something to do with Jesus' saying in

24:42–44. They are not independent stories, but are part of the broader perspective to explain what Jesus' saying was about. This set of parables serves as the climax among parables in Matthew as Jesus went to face his executioners shortly after he taught them. This set of parables also fit into Matthew's eschatological discourse.

The plot is simple, and the story is short. Jesus contrasted two different kinds of slaves in 24:45–51. The contrasting stories have the same plot line. Both start with the statement about the kind of slave working for the owner (24:45, 48). In 24:45, Jesus began his story with a question instead of a statement, as if to challenge his listeners to be a good slave. The good slave was faithful and wise. Faithfulness denotes being true to his duty. The "wise" slave would apply the character of dutifulness to his skills so that his performance would be true to the assigned task. Thus, he was not generally good but specifically good in character and skills. Both good character and skills resulted in greater responsibility (implying possibly greater power and reward) in 24:47.

The story however focuses on the evil slave as a hypothesis of what could happen.[1] In 24:48, Jesus described the slave as being evil, depraved in his character. The story shows the evil proceeding from the slave's heart in 24:49 by showing the conversation the slave had with himself. The literal rendering of the Greek is "he said in his heart." This internal conversation comes from Jesus the omniscient narrator to illustrate the hopeless character flaw of this slave. Even his intentions were evil, evident in his action in 24:49. His action consisted of violence and debauchery. The violence shown here was most inexcusable because it was against a fellow slave. In Jesus' time, only owners were allowed to commit violence against slaves (e.g., the subsequent punishment of the evil slave in 24:51). Slaves probably were allowed to exercise some violence towards their subordinate slaves, but Jesus used "fellow slaves" to convey the equality of the evil slave with other slaves. The evil slave then overtook his lot in life. His debauchery resembled the Greco-Roman aristocratic feasts. He then violated convention in a horrible way by acting like the owner himself, perhaps driven by

1. The Greek word for "if" in 24:48 indicates a third-class condition, a condition of hypothesis. In other words, Jesus was not saying this second part was a hypothesis. This is what modern people call a "what if." E.g., "If the girl says yes, you must make sure you have clothing for a date." The third-class condition indicates the possibility of something happening in the future. The slave had a choice in the future as to whether to treat the master as if he had gone for a long time, thus allowing unruly behavior to take place. The slave did not have to be this way as he anticipated the future, but in the story, he gave in.

his false view of himself. The result was shocking because the owner caught him unaware in 24:50–51. The translation in 24:51 can be puzzling. One translation (NIV) calls the punishment "cut into pieces" with murderous implications. However, how can someone who was literally cut into pieces be sent to a place of hypocrites? Perhaps "cutting to pieces" actually means being severely flogged by a whip cutting across the body. The description is vividly painful. In colloquial parlance, the owner beat the living daylight out of him and ripped him like a newspaper. Thus, what he had done to his fellow slaves, he now received. He was then alienated from the household by being thrown together with other hypocrites. Formerly, he loaded himself with food and drink within the household. Now, he would be cut off from such luxury, forever living outside.

The assignment to hypocrites also deserves some thinking. The owner's assignment of the bad slave to the place where hypocrites belonged indicates the kind of crime committed. Hypocrites were people who would not do what they were supposed to but pretended that they were better than they really were. In the same way, the evil slave was not doing what he was supposed to, but pretended that he was in a higher position. In some ways, he was much like the hypocrites. Thus, the punishment fit the crime.

The parable has some important traits. Jesus used an internal conversation in this evildoer's heart. This internal conversation is a good device to show the main issue that caused the subsequent folly. The content of the conversation shows that the reason why the slave did evil was because of how long the owner had been absent. Thus, the delay of the owner's eventual arrival was part of the cause for his behavior of not keeping watch (cf. 25:5). He thought that the master would never find out. Another perspective comes from understanding the background. The slave's problem was his complete violation of his own position by behaving as if he were the owner in 24:49. Thus the slave's identity should have restricted his behavior to that which would confirm to the social norm. He received back the exact consequences of his behavior.

Now, we should interpret this parable based on 24:42–44. Jesus talked about alertness for the thief who would break in. The same analogy could be applied to the coming of the Lord in 24:42. Jesus added more dimensions by speaking the parable. We must notice that the entire parable coheres well with Jesus' saying because both talk about suffering harm. The thief's break-in would have caused damage to the household. Thus, the owner would keep alert to keep from suffering harm. The master's return in the parable would however cause the slave harm. So, what did Jesus mean when he spoke about not keeping watch? Based on his sayings here, it means that the person did not know his identity. It further means that this person did not think that the master would see what he did because the master delayed his coming. It also means that the household would suffer from the person's dereliction of duty. Thus, the idea of keeping watch does not mean not sleeping because the saying about the thief was just Jesus' analogy. It does not mean to do more for the kingdom either. Jesus did not take the "more the better" approach. Instead, Jesus focused on the identity of the slave who was supposed to know his normal duty. In other words, keeping watch means to do exactly what one is supposed to do based on an understanding of personal identity.

I told the story backwards by taking out the bad guy. Everyone wants a good ending with the good guy. We want everyone to get along and have no one rejected for any reason. Reality is different. The first-century ideal is that all slaves should obey their masters. It is not a choice for the slave, as the law legislated that slaves were obligated as chattel of their masters. I told the story based on Roman laws commonly accepted by both owners and those who served them. The slave who lazed around would be the one at risk. This slave took calculated risks, but did not realize that his calculation was off. The ending was violent and scary.

Matthew had given this kind of violent ending as in 13:42, 50, 22:13, and 25:30, showing this type of parable to be similar in gravity to those passages. This formula by Jesus has repeated so much by now among Matthew's listeners that they would have been quite familiar at this point. The parable served as the severest of warnings to Jesus' disciples, a warning they had to heed or risk grave eschatological consequences. At the end, the entire parable answers the initial question the disciples asked in 24:3. Jesus answered in a roundabout way by telling them that they were incorrect to ask about the timing. They were to focus more on *how* they were to prepare. In short, while the disciples focused on "when" (cf. 24:3) Jesus would come, Jesus refocused them on "how" they should live. The entire parable answered the queries of the disciples.

PUTTING THE TEXT IN HISTORY:
MEANINGS FOR THE WORLD OF AUTHOR-READERS

Matthew's audience, like the early church faith communities, faced an incredible amount of challenges. Part of their belief system must have something to do with Jesus' second coming. While many might mock them that Jesus had not been resurrected from the dead, the lack of evidence of the second coming should result in the next level of humiliation. They probably asked the same question the disciples did about when the Son of Man would come back.

Equally pressing were the injustices all around, especially the frustrating injustices against the Jewish nation in the removal of the temple. When would Jesus come back to right the wrong? Matthew's answer would not be most helpful for those seeking certainty. The question would not be answered directly or even indirectly (cf. 24:36), as certainty would be impossible. Instead, Matthew redirected the attention of his audience to focus more on their position in the kingdom with the repeated motif of the slave's identity. The message to them would say, "Why ask about *when* the second coming is? Why not focus more on *who* you are and do what you are supposed to do?"

By translating this discourse, Matthew sought to resolve the irresolvable questions of his time. To Matthew, the right question is as important as asking any question. The right question in this parable is about who the kingdom citizen is in relation to the Lord. The answer comes from doing and not from speaking.

The parable is highly important for the faith community of today. As people did in the days of Jesus and Matthew, some people in the faith community today also focus on "when" Jesus will come back. Radio personality Harold Camping has been making numerous predictions about Jesus' second coming. Non-Christian versions focus on the Mayan calendar and Nostradamus. Jesus' teaching is clear. He wanted his followers to focus on being who they were called to be rather than the time of the apocalypse. The situation today shows that modern believers are not all that different from the disciples. People tend to focus on *when* while Jesus wanted to focus on the *how*. However, Matthew wanted to warn his audience that the longer the owner was gone, the greater the slave might misunderstand his real position. The prideful behavior of many, then, is the result of ignoring the real place of the Coming One in favor of self-aggrandizement.

The homiletical possibilities are rich in this short and straightforward parable. Jesus repeated the position of the two slaves. The text shows the contrast of good-slave / bad-slave. This is the simple contrast of the story. The parable emphasized the bad slave by talking about him more so that his listeners would be like the good slave.

Title: Not When but How!
Telling it Backward: The two slaves await the return of the owner. They faithfully serve because they know they are slaves . . . but Jesus told a different story. What if people know that Jesus would return?

1) The Good Slave (24:45–47)
2) The Bad Slave (24:48–51)
Conclusion: Not when the Son of Man is coming but how the followers prepare (cf. 24:1–3). They must prepare as if he really would return.

REFLECTION QUESTIONS

1.   What was the original intent of the parable?

2.   Why did Jesus start with a question in 24:45?

3.   What similar problem do we face, as did the disciples back in the days of Jesus and Matthew?

4.   What does the harsh conclusion tell us about Jesus' emphasis?

5.   Why would the bad slave end up with the hypocrites? What are the similarities between the two?

6.   Why did Jesus focus more on the bad slave than the good?

13

Be Wise. Know Your Place!

TELLING IT BACKWARD: MATTHEW 25:1-13

Jesus said, "At that time the kingdom of heaven will be like ten virgins who took their lamps and went out to meet the bridegroom. Knowing how the arrival of the bridegroom could be uncertain, all of them exercised precaution to bring extra oil with them. When the bridegroom was delayed a long time, they all became drowsy and fell asleep. But at midnight there was a shout, 'Look, the bridegroom is here! Come out to meet him.' Then all the virgins woke up and trimmed their lamps. The bridegroom arrived, and they all went inside with him to the wedding banquet. Then the door was shut. Therefore stay alert, because you do not know the day or the hour."

My story has a happy ending. Who doesn't like a story with happy ending? Weddings should have happy endings. Yet, every culture has its own wedding rituals. In dealing with ethnic Chinese culture, westerners should be aware of many taboos. For example, the number "four" sounds like "death" in Cantonese. That is not a number one wants to mutter in a Cantonese-style wedding. People who can afford the banquet usually give cash or check in red envelopes at the guest-book signing table before all guests enter the banquet hall. These affairs are ten-course meals complete with the rice dish at the end. Usually, the rice dish is a formality no one bothers much with, but it does convey the hospitality of having leftover so that every single guest, including the most gluttonous one, would be satisfied. Clothing colors also mean something in Asian cultures. For example, in Indian weddings, guests should avoid wearing black (the mourning color) or white (the funeral color). Unlike western weddings, no guest would dare to dance or ask for a dance with the bride. The fact is, weddings are rites of passage for couples to create a new family in every culture. The rituals that involve the couple matter. People involved would adhere carefully to these meaningful rituals.

By now, in Matthew's narrative of Jesus' parables, the banqueting theme is prominent and eschatological. This parable, as a part of the eschatological discourse, contains a very serious message. In the days of Jesus, the bride's party usually accompanied the procession that climaxed at the banquet. Some see these virgins as bridesmaids. Whether or not they were the modern equivalent of bridesmaids, these virgins were to be part of the wedding. Missing it, based on the result, would be a huge social faux pas. The story I told backward above indicates a perfect scenario. Yet, neither Jesus nor Matthew told the story in this backward fashion. This story is exactly about faux pas.

TELLING IT NORMAL: KEY ELEMENTS IN THE STORY

"At that time the kingdom of heaven will be like ten virgins who took their lamps and went out to meet the bridegroom. 2 Five of the virgins were foolish, and five were wise. 3 When the foolish ones took their lamps, they did not take extra olive oil with them. 4 But the wise ones took flasks of olive oil with their lamps. 5 When the bridegroom was delayed a long time, they all became drowsy and fell asleep. 6 But at midnight there was a shout, 'Look, the bridegroom is here! Come out to meet him.' 7 Then all the virgins woke up and trimmed their lamps. 8 The foolish ones said to the wise, 'Give us some of your oil, because our lamps are going out.' 9 'No,' they replied. 'There won't be enough for you and for us. Go instead to those who sell oil and buy some for yourselves.' 10 But while they had gone to buy it, the bridegroom arrived, and those who were ready went inside with him to the wedding banquet. Then the door was shut. 11 Later, the other virgins came too, saying, 'Lord, lord! Let us in!' 12 But he replied, replied, 'I tell you the truth, I do not know you!' 13 Therefore stay alert, because you do not know the day or the hour."

Right at the start of this story, Jesus said, "At that time . . . ." This chronological marker points to the same event Jesus had been discussing all along since Matthew 24. Furthermore, this chronological marker refers back to the previous parable, a story about what would happen when the sudden arrival of the owner. Thus, the story is really another explanation of broader teachings such as 24:3, 14, 43, evident in the conclusion of 25:13, but we are jumping ahead.

Jesus did not hesitate to state the problem of the story in a deductive manner. Right away, he categorized the virgins into foolish and wise. The order of the story focuses on the foolish ones. What does being foolish mean? In the New Testament, it could mean being stupid. It could also mean someone who did not exercise prudence to cause the best outcome. The outcome could be moral or practical. The English word "moron" came from this word in Greek, apparently stressing the intelligence aspect. However, Jesus' story seems to emphasize a lack of prudence. What does being wise mean? Quite often, in the New Testament, wise means someone who either had rightly applied skills or had the right character of being mindful. The story seems to emphasize the second aspect, the mindfulness.

Jesus pointedly stated the problem: some were wise and others were foolish. The single indicator was the way they prepared for the arrival of the groom as an analogy of the Son of Man.[1] The coming of the Son of Man would be like the coming of the bridegroom. Both demanded alertness and preparedness. Awareness of appropriate preparation is the key, both for the previous parable about the slave and this parable. The fools took the lamps without taking any oil. The wise took along extra oil. It is important to note that alertness had nothing to do with whether they were sleeping. Rather, it had much to do with preparedness. Obviously, they expected the groom to come way before but the groom did not come. By the time the groom came, it was the middle of the night.

The unprepared virgins asked those prepared virgins to share, but the latter did not have enough. Thus, by the time the foolish virgins had what they needed for the procession, the banquet hall's doors were closed. The groom told them that he did not know them. This final fate had them excluded from the household. Their cry "Lord, lord" sounds the same as those whom Jesus did not know in 7:22–23.[2] The parallel could have been

1. 25:3 starts with "for when" in Greek, indicating the very reason why these virgins were fools in Jesus' eyes: they were not prepared.

2. "Saying" in 25:11 is in present tense in Greek, indicating a continuous plea such

quite deliberate. In 7:23, Jesus called those excluded "evil." Here, these were called "fools." The fools and evil people shared the same fate. The Lord did not know them, and they were excluded from the kingdom. We must be quite careful to note that the kingdom here excluded such people. To be excluded was a serious matter in the ancient household. Such alienation meant that excluded people would not share all the blessings and benefits of the household. Most western readers probably would say, "What's the big deal?" As stated earlier, the situation in Jesus' world demanded the virgins to be vigilant or the groom would be greatly insulted to the degree of refusing to associate with the unprepared wedding guests.

Some interpreters want to allegorize each part, giving the lamps symbolic meanings, etc. This ploy is unnecessary in that Jesus already said that the kingdom was like the entire story, and not its individual parts. The story also shows the power structure of Jesus' society. The groom was never faulted for his tardiness because the occasion was centered on him. The foolish were entirely condemned for not anticipating his tardiness. The very same power structure existed in the previous parable about the delayed master and the wicked slave. In this way, the power structure of the story informs the disciples not only of the need to be alert, but also the basis on which the alertness was built. It is important not to allegorize Jesus as the groom or the master and so on, but we can say that the value system of the kingdom is analogized to the power relationship illustrated here. Within that power structure, Jesus would reign supreme whether his coming was delayed or not. The followers needed to prepare with alertness because they ought to recognize their place in the overall scheme of Jesus' coming.

When reading the story backward in my previous section, I told the story in the societal norm. In the story Jesus told, the virgins went against the norm and paid for it. Jesus used a societal norm, not to illustrate how right such norms were. Surely, Jesus would not have advocated throwing people out today if he were to be eating with us. Jesus was not advocating the action of the groom, but was telling the story to say that the kingdom had a norm (i.e., "the kingdom of heaven will be like . . ."). The kingdom was not a free-for-all. Its members had to play by the rules.

The meaning of the parable cannot be complete without reading the story as part of 24:42–44. The vocabulary of 24:42–44 parallels with 25:6. The context within Matthew indicates that the evil slave here would relate

as, "Please please please, let us in. We are really sorry . . ." in succession. The decisive response of the rejecting groom seems to convey this message, "No matter what vocabulary and how urgent or long your plea is, you will never be part of my household celebration."

well with the evil people back in 27:23 who also were rejected harshly. The discussion about the coming of the Son of Man in 24:42–44 points towards the eschatological climax Jesus was teaching. Such a climax would be fitting in light of Jesus' first discourse in Matthew in 7:22–23. The idea of judgment started in Matthew 7 and ended here with a clearer vision of the Son of Man's second coming. More important is the similarity between 7:22–23 and 24:11: those who professed the "Lord" were condemned. In other words, mere verbal profession without any real substance would not be good enough for Jesus. The emphasis on the power of the master and the groom sufficiently informed the disciples of the need to recognize the power of the one returning. No one should take such a power for granted.

PUTTING THE TEXT IN HISTORY: MEANINGS FOR THE WORLD OF AUTHOR-READERS

The story about the ten virgins must mean something to Matthew's audience. With the destruction of the temple in 70 CE, they literally saw Jesus' prophecy in 24:1–2 flash before their eyes, they had to have questions about when exactly the Son of Man would return. Based on 24:24, 38, Jesus' coming would seem to be swift, but Matthew's community lived in tension because Jesus made those pronouncements some forty years ago, and the end was nowhere to be found. With the passing destruction of the temple, they would think that the second part of Jesus' prophecy about himself would come swiftly. With some of the tension and pressure facing Matthew's community, some of its members would ask questions about when the Son of Man would come back. After all, so much prophecy had been proven correct. Would the coming of the Son of Man be immediate?

Matthew's story of Jesus' parable should make a strong ethical impact. Matthew's community faced some ethical challenges. Some members could well say that the coming of the Son of Man would allow them to just sit back and relax. Others could have experienced the delay as a cause of failure to be alert. Matthew's story addressed those who thought that sitting back was the answer because they were to keep alert by due diligence much like those who were to prepare for the wedding banquet. The preparedness allowed them to carry on their daily routine including sleeping. Matthew also addressed those who might have completely forgotten about the coming of the Son of Man. The parable served as a warning to those lax members about the real need to take what Jesus said seriously. They should make the diligent choice. These stories Matthew recorded seem to be eschatological discourses, but when set in context of Matthew's situation, they became rhetorical channel to ethics.

One aspect of the parable of the virgins should stand out for modern faith communities. We moderns tend to associate wisdom with IQ but Matthew's Jesus had a different measuring stick. Matthew's Jesus measured wisdom by the way the faith community responded to the Son of Man, especially his eschatological work. The parable showed that there was indeed a "norm" in the kingdom in the same way a wedding procedure had a norm. Mere profession of the words "Lord, Lord" is not enough. Is there any norm in our pluralistic world? Matthew's Jesus would have answered in the positive. But in what way? I think the answer would be better answered by asking another question. Does accepting the Son of Man's second coming make a difference in the Christian community's life? It should. What makes the difference though? It seems that the power hierarchy of the kingdom found in both the previous parable of the evil slaves and this parable shows that the key is the recognition of who the Son of Man really is. If everything revolves around his interest rather than each community member's self-interest, then the parable would make a difference in the community and in the world. The "wise" virgins always recognize the power of the groom and live accordingly.

The homiletical nuance required of this simple text should be noted. The power of the groom (as a parallel to the previous evil slave metaphor) deserves attention. Our democratic mind may reject the idea of power and want to read the parable as mere failure of duty, but the pairing of the parables will challenge our modern sensibilities. If we are accountable to a higher power, we would naturally become more alert.

Title: Be Wise. Know Your Place!
Telling It Backward: Everyone recognizes the importance of the groom and acts accordingly . . . but Jesus speaks of a different reality. What if the Lord's return is a surprise?

1) The Foolish Virgins (25:3, 8–10)
2) The Wise Virgins (25:4)
3) The Result: No amount of proclamation of "Lord, Lord" will save the fools.
Conclusion: What if the Lord's return is a surprise? The wise recognize the Lord's authority and stay alert.

REFLECTION QUESTIONS

1. What are the definitions of wisdom and folly?

2. Does alertness mean the virgins do not sleep?

3. What does alertness mean?

4. How does the saying of "Lord, Lord" illustrate Matthew's greater points elsewhere?

5. What is the root of alertness?

14

Production by "Talent"?

Jesus told this story: "For it is like a man going on a journey, who summoned his slaves and entrusted his property to them. To one he gave five talents, to another two, and to another one, each according to his ability. Then he went on his journey. The one who had received five talents went off right away and put his money to work and gained five more. In the same way, the one who had two gained two more. And the one who had received one talent went out and gained one. After a long time, the master of those slaves came and settled his accounts with them. The one who had received the five talents came and brought five more, saying, 'Sir, you entrusted me with five talents. See, I have gained five more.' His master answered, 'Well done, good and faithful slave! You have been faithful in a few things. I will put you in charge of many things. Enter into the joy of your master.' The one with the two talents also came and said, 'Sir, you entrusted two talents to me. See, I have gained two more.' His master answered, 'Well done, good and faithful slave! You have been faithful with a few things. I will put you in charge of many things. Enter into the joy of your master.' Then the one who had received the one talent came and said, 'Sir, I have made one more talent by giving it to someone to generate some interest.' His master answered, 'Well done, good and faithful slave! You have been faithful with a few things. I will put you in charge of many things. Enter into the joy of your master.'"

THIS PARABLE HAS BEEN interpreted variously. A most common interpretation is to see this as a discussion on talent or, even more specifically, spiritual gifts. Most likely, this understanding of "talents" as a measurement of currency is unduly influenced by the English translation "talents" as a description of one's aptitude. Such readings are muddled by bad hermeneutics because such interpreters do not take into consideration of wider discourse context of Matthew 24 and 25. There is no discussion about talents or spiritual gifts. So, let us try our best to put aside the popular interpretation (even among reputable commentators) for a second. The fact is, "talents" is a term used for measuring the weight of money. It has nothing to do with a person's aptitude. The story is not so much about using spiritual gifts but is more about the kind of attitude one should have when faced with the prospect of the second coming. Later discussion will also elaborate on possible implications of Jesus' parable about stewardship here. This parable is a continuation of the ten-virgin parable and it serves as a logical follow-up to the last parables about alertness.

Under all ideal circumstances, the above backward telling of the story would make perfect sense. By now, all of Matthew's master-slave parables should have the same plot. The master gave the slaves something to do. The slaves should do the tasks. In doing so, the slaves would be fulfilling their most basic requirement. If the master decided to be gracious, they would receive due recognition. We all wish the story were just that simple, but just about every master-slave parable has its own twists. The present parable is no exception and does not adhere to my backward story above.

TELLING IT NORMAL: KEY ELEMENTS IN THE STORY

14 "For it is like a man going on a journey, who summoned his slaves and entrusted his property to them. 15 To one he gave five talents, to another two, and to another one, each according to his ability. Then he went on his journey. 16 The one who had received five talents went off right away and put his money to work and gained five more. 17 In the same way, the one who had two gained two more. 18 But the one who had received one talent went out and dug a hole in the ground and hid his master's money in it. 19 After a long time, the master of those slaves came and settled his accounts with them. 20 The one who had received the five talents came and brought five more, saying, 'Sir, you entrusted me with five talents. See, I have gained five more.' 21 His master answered,

'Well done, good and faithful slave! You have been faithful in a few things. I will put you in charge of many things. Enter into the joy of your master.' 22 The one with the two talents also came and said, 'Sir, you entrusted two talents to me. See, I have gained two more.' 23 His master answered, 'Well done, good and faithful slave! You have been faithful with a few things. I will put you in charge of many things. Enter into the joy of your master.' 24 Then the one who had received the one talent came and said, 'Sir, I knew that you were a hard man, harvesting where you did not sow, and gathering where you did not scatter seed, 25 so I was afraid, and I went and hid your talent in the ground. See, you have what is yours.' 26 But his master answered, 'Evil and lazy slave! So you knew that I harvest where I didn't sow and gather where I didn't scatter? 27 Then you should have deposited my money with the bankers, and on my return I would have received my money back with interest! 28 Therefore take the talent from him and give it to the one who has ten. 29 For the one who has will be given more, and he will have more than enough. But the one who does not have, even what he has will be taken from him. 30 And throw that worthless slave into the outer darkness, where there will be weeping and gnashing of teeth.'"

One of the funniest recent pictures I saw was a picture of politicians sleeping through their open sessions. I do not recall whether it was the British Parliament or the US Congress. Most likely, there have been several such pictures of both bodies circulating the internet. All I remember is the picture of various politicians in a deep coma while their colleagues argued their case. Such a picture shows the lax approach some people take towards their duty. The humorous picture is very similar to the ending of this story. Only this story does not have a humorous ending.

This is yet one more "the kingdom of heaven is like . . ." parable. The entire parable analogizes the kingdom. The metaphorical force that leads to a message should somehow answer two questions. First, how is this message logically related to 24:45—25:13? Second, how is the message related to the greater question and answer of 24:3-4? To understand this parable, we start with its storyline first.

The main problem of 25:14-30 is the departure of master in 25:14. The slaves he summoned would be entrusted with his finances. To the first one, the owner gave roughly a little less than one year's salary. To the second one, he gave roughly less than half of the first. To the third one, he gave half the amount of the second slave's. The property owner gave each slave according to his ability to make profit from the finance. The parable does not speak explicitly of the motive for profits but the results clearly indicate the expectation to make a profit. The first two slaves doubled the amount given to them. The last slave who received less had done nothing. Jesus set the pattern of the parable to be about profits, and then he broke the pattern by talking about the unfaithful slave in 25:18. This unfaithful slave did not bother to make a profit.

The day of reckoning came when the master surprisingly came home in 25:19. The two "good and faithful" slaves would both double their profit. The evil and lazy slave did not. The lazy slave's conversation with the owner is telling because it makes no sense. If the owner were as harsh as he stated in 25:24–25, would he not work harder to gain even more profit instead of burying the amount? In other words, if the slave believed his own excuse, wouldn't he work hard to gain something? The owner's statement in 25:27 shows that in the owner's mind, the slave really did not believe what he said, making him a hypocrite and a liar who was full of excuses. The owner's description of the bad slave was not merely "stupid" but "evil and lazy." The problem then was not that the slave had absolutely no ability. He obviously had some abilities. According to the owner, the origin of the problem was the slave's evil and lazy character. While the word for "evil" actually points towards morality, the word for "lazy" points towards integrity. His evilness came from the excuse he used but did not believe. His problem then was not the lack of intelligence but the lack of moral fiber and character. Thus, the owner answered the last slave according to his understanding of the owner's character and punished him accordingly. The owner then rewarded the most faithful slave with the portion of the lazy slave, and punished the lazy slave with expulsion into the darkness. The lazy slave's fate would ensure that he would have none of the protection and benefits of belonging to the owner's household. He would be essentially homeless.

Jesus' parable would offend modern sensibilities due to its violent nature. Yet, Jesus' language was much in accordance with the convention back then. Slaves were chattel whose own existence was based on their productivity and the owner's good will. A slave who failed to profit the owner had forfeited his place in the household. The expulsion of this slave would be something like the modern lazy worker being fired in a tough economy. The story had no happy ending.

What message does this parable carry, just from its above plot line? Some people mistakenly think that the message is "use it or lose it." Instead, the message seems to be "grow it or lose it." The message seems very simple. The slave's social location required him to fulfill his duty the best he could, much like the way the slave of 24:45 or the five wise virgins in 25:4. There is absolutely no reason for not doing his duty because the large sum given to each slave was impossibly large, at least quite a bit larger than the amount most Galileans were used to. Now, isn't this really the point? Whatever the master gave was enormously valuable. In an analogical way, those who possessed the kingdom message ought to see the stewardship as something impossibly valuable, much like having just gained a stewardship of a large sum of money.

At the general level, Jesus appeared to be talking about the stewardship of the kingdom because of the verbal parallel between 25:29 and 13:12. The parallel words show that the presupposition for understanding 25:29 must be an understanding of the parable of the sower in Matthew 13. Ironically, Jesus used an enormous financial sum, something the Galilean peasant longed for, to illustrate what they actually needed to do to prepare for God's real work. What "word" of the kingdom did Jesus teach in this specific situation? Surely, we cannot stop at the general level of Matthew 13. Up to this point, Jesus defined the required alertness for those facing the delay of second coming as dutifulness. The idea of duty will become clearer when we read the conclusive remarks in the parable of sheep and goats. For now, as long as we notice the importance of the theme of duty and the value of Jesus' "word," we are on the right track.

How does the parable logically relate to the previous two parables in 24:45—25:13? Both the previous parables contain the idea of a delay (24:48; 25:5). The previous two parables had the theme of surprised visit from the one holding power (24:43; 25:13) but the present parable does not. In line with the previous two parables, this parable also has the plot of delay in 25:19, linking well with Jesus' original discourse in 24:3–4. The element of unexpected visit probably ought to be assumed in this present parable due to the similar element of delay. Based on all that Jesus said before, the surprising visit should not be as shocking. At this point, the text implicitly asks the readers, "Why would anyone who believes in the teaching of Matthew 24 not expect the coming of the Son of Man?" Jesus did not seem to state very explicitly that the delay would happen, but he wanted the disciples to keep in mind the answers to the question, "What if the second coming were delayed?" What attitude should the disciples have facing the uncertain timing of the second coming? This parable shares an additional similarity with 24:51 in its ending of 25:30. The two parables are similarly harsh. The following structure will summarize what I just said above.

Parable	Absence	Fulfillment or Neglect	Rejection	Conclusion
Virgins	25:1–5 (Groom)	25:6–10	25:11–12	25:13
Talents	25:14–18 (Master)	25:19–25	25:26–28	25:29–30

Reading them as the same type of parable, we cannot help coming to the conclusion that Jesus' words were full of warnings and vitriol not just addressing his disciples, but also polemicizing against the temple. We should not forget what Jesus said in 24:2. As previous discussions have already pointed out, the temple was going to meet destruction much like the withering fig tree. Jesus reiterated in 24:15 the horrible fate that would eventually befall the temple. These are all harsh sayings. The gospel and the heavenly kingdom had never looked so glum. These served as warning passages about the disciples' duty.

In my backward telling of the story, if the community were to function properly, the backward telling of the story would have been the norm. All members would do their duty based on their assigned lot because even the one with the least amount possessed an enormous amount of money. If not, let the temple destruction be the warning of destructive fate. In reality, Jesus deemed a neglect of duty by the disciple to be as impossible as the slave who did nothing with what he got. The true disciple would always fulfill his duty to the word with which he had been entrusted much like a good slave would in his society. The reason why he would fulfill the duty was not only because the master was over him but also because he was entrusted with stuff of great worth. As the master told the last slave, even if the slave took the easiest route, he would still gain. In other words, the disciples ought to see kingdom stewardship as a win-win situation. The concluding parable of the sheep and goats will prove that my conclusion is correct.

PUTTING THE TEXT IN HISTORY: MEANINGS FOR THE WORLD OF AUTHOR-READERS

Matthew's community had to face pressure. The pressure to conform was great. Within all the changes, Matthew's community could choose to coast and live an easier life or face the music and buckle up for a rough ride.

Matthew's Jesus encouraged them to face the eschatological music and march to a different drumbeat.

The community had to use the temple destruction as a moment of contemplation about the promises of Jesus. If Jesus were true to his promise of judgment and the temple judgment had already come to pass, then the parable would become a stern warning for them not to be lax in their faith. Instead, they had to look at what their duty would be in this new era of second-generation Christ followers. The entire book written by Matthew was the means for them to reflect. For each generation of Christ followers, the same questions would plague them, "Who are we? What are we doing here?" With Matthew's stern stories, no one should take it for granted that a pat answer has been provided. The journey continued for Matthew's community. Identity formation is an ongoing process.

When writing this chapter, I ran across an article claiming that about half of all American Christians believe that Jesus will come back in the next forty years.[1] While statistics can mislead, this statistic poses a strong challenge in light of the parables. Matthew's Jesus told some very harsh parables, and all such parables ended in judgment. These parables were no joke. If half of the Christian in the US believe Jesus will come back in forty years, I wonder if they understand what these parables are really teaching. Matthew's Jesus taught the group of disciples against the backdrop of the temple. The temple had not served its function and faced grave danger. The disciples who would become the new community would carry on its duty. I wonder how many of the believers in the statistics have seriously thought about their duty or have taken for granted that they are already doing their duty. Perhaps, not many in Jesus' day thought about what Jesus had said either. For the twenty-first century believer, we could be playing the same song with a different DJ today. The parables surely addressed the inactive stargazing (not to mention the *Left Behind* reading) mentality of many in the modern faith community.

It is no easy task to preach this passage because its tone is extremely stern. Even the master is stern. While we may be careful not to analogize the master to be either God or Jesus, we cannot avoid the conclusion that the kingdom of heaven required its citizens to be wholly responsible. The whole story was about responsibility for one's lot in the kingdom.

---

1. http://www.huffingtonpost.com/2013/04/01/christ-second-coming-survey_n_2993218.html?ncid=edlinkusaolp00000009, accessed April 1, 2013.

Title: Production by "Talent"?
Telling It Backward: Every slave works according to his ability
to produce comparable goods. The master is happy . . . but
Jesus speaks of a different reality. Is there such a thing as a non-
productive slave?

1) The Good Slaves and Rewards (25:14–23)
2) The Bad Slave and Punishment (25:24–30)
Conclusion: Not about talent but about moral character (24:26); not about
what you have but what you do with what you have (25:28–29); not just
about any trust but about an enormously valuable trust that was a guar-
anteed winner; not just about individuals but about the faith community
(24:4). There is no such thing as a non-productive faith community.

REFLECTION QUESTIONS

1. What is the implication of Jesus' slave stories?

2. Why is the saying of the owner in 25:26 significant in understanding
   the main issue?

3. How is this story related to the temple?

4. How is this story related to the previous two? Similarities? Differences?

5. How does this story speak to Matthew's audience?

6. How does the story speak to today's faith community?

15

Deceiving Appearance

> "When the Son of Man comes in his *glory* and all the angels with him, then he will sit on his *glorious* throne. All the nations will be assembled before him, and he will separate people one from another like a shepherd separates the sheep from the goats. The shepherd will keep both because they are both clean animals that are useful for his purpose."

LABELING AND SEPARATION PERVADE human existence. Separation from the "other" ensures our own place in the "in crowd." Do we notice that in our PC world, labeling is almost taboo? Not so the place where I grew up. I grew up in the New South where white kids would tell me to stick to my own kind (i.e., Asians) when it came to asking girls out. Some went as far as to utter the N-word as if it was normal. Do we notice that labeling and stereotyping still go on, though? In a lot of Hollywood movies, the villain has a foreign accent (e.g., Arabic or Asian or European) and sometimes dresses differently (e.g., a turban). In certain genres (e.g., action movies) an American accent automatically qualifies one to be the "good guy." The desire for reassurance of one's place in this world often turns into alienation of someone different than we are, whether the boundary line is skin color, accent, ethnicity, citizenship, or even sexual orientation. Jesus' world also had some boundary lines to separate people: rich/poor; Jews/gentiles; pure/profane; Greeks/barbarians; etc.

Some have considered this not so much a parable but an analogy of Jesus' final conclusion, but the dramatic element is so strong and conversations so vivid that we must classify it as a parable. After all, how do we talk to sheep and goats? Many Sunday school teachers would portray the goats negatively in their retelling of the story. However, we need another look because sheep and goats were kosher animals in Jesus' day. There is no indicator that goats were viewed negatively in Jesus' day. A normal shepherd would have kept both for the benefits of farming. Yet, neither Jesus nor Matthew told the story in this backward fashion. Jesus told this story in a distinct way to conclude his discourse about the temple and the disciples.

TELLING IT NORMAL: KEY ELEMENTS IN THE STORY

31 "When the Son of Man comes in his *glory* and all the angels with him, then he will sit on his *glorious* throne. 32 All the nations will be assembled before him, and he will separate people one from another like a shepherd separates the sheep from the goats. 33 He will put the sheep on his right and the goats on his left. 34 Then the king will say to those on his right, 'Come, you who are blessed by my Father, inherit the kingdom prepared for you from the foundation of the world. 35 For I was hungry and you gave me food, I was thirsty and you gave me something to drink, I was a stranger and you invited me in, 36 I was naked and you gave me clothing, I was sick and you took care of me, I was in prison and you visited me.' 37 Then the righteous will answer him, 'Lord, when did we see you hungry and feed you, or thirsty and give you something to drink? 38 When did we see you a stranger and invite you in, or naked and clothe you? 39 When did we see you sick or in prison and visit you?' 40 And the king will answer them, 'I tell you the truth, just as you did it for one of the least of these brothers or sisters of mine, you did it for me.'

41 "Then he will say to those on his left, 'Depart from me, you accursed, into the eternal fire that has been prepared for the devil and his angels! 42 For I was hungry and you gave me nothing to eat, I was thirsty and you gave me nothing to drink. 43 I was a stranger and you did not receive me as a guest, naked and you did not clothe me, sick and in prison and you did not visit me.' 44 Then they too will answer, 'Lord, when did we see you hungry or thirsty

> or a stranger or naked or sick or in prison, and did not give you
> whatever you needed?' 45 Then he will answer them, 'I tell you the
> truth, just as you did not do it for one of the least of these, you did
> not do it for me.' 46 And these will depart into eternal punishment,
> but the righteous into eternal life."

This conclusive remark headed by the parable was Jesus' way of lowering the boom on his followers with a sideways glance at the temple institution. This parable is spectacular in that it differs from another similar parable in 13:24–30. In the parable of the wheat and weeds in 13:24–30, only the wheat would be considered useable in Jesus' world. Closer, but not quite the same, is the story of different kinds of fish in 13:47–52 where the same word for "separate" occurs in both places (cf. 13:49; 25:32). Here, both the sheep and goats were kosher. Interpreters need to keep in mind the issue of similarity between the two when reading this parable. I shall deal with this issue later.

We still need to answer the question why the sheep and goats, two similarly kosher animals, were categorized in such extreme terms. After all, there is little evidence, if any at all, in the first century literature that goats, often pastured together with sheep, were all that bad. Jesus was saying that these two were very similar. Both had ritually clean traits, but only one inherited the kingdom. In view of the temple religion, Jesus used these two animals to say that true and false religions could appear quite similar. Only when people examined how the two treated others, in light of the kingdom Jesus established, were true and false followers separated.

The parable intertwines with Jesus' teaching throughout the passage of 25:31–46. The section 25:32–33 contains the simple and bare-bones part of the parable. While the saying is very simple, the shepherd surprisingly separated the sheep and the goats, representing "all the nations." Some might see "all nations" as an exclusive label for gentiles, but 24:14 allows for inclusion of both Jews and gentiles. In the early church (if we read 24:9 in that context), the opponents included both parties. The early church mission also embraced both Jews and gentiles, as we read the so-called Great Commission of 28:18–20 where the phrase "all nations" occurs. In the story of the sheep and goats, the shepherd took on the role of the king in 25:34–46. Who then was this king? We cannot avoid comparison of this with the Son of Man because he would be the one sitting on the throne in 25:31. If this were the case and sheep and goats also represented two kinds of people, then this parable acts like an allegory with each character representing someone. Strictly speaking, this is probably the only parable in Matthew that plays the role of an allegory.

The allegory is highly moralistic. In accordance to Jewish convention of his day, Jesus signified those on the right of the king to be the "good guys" and those on the left the "bad guys." Interestingly, both parties were not limited to Jews, but representing all nations. Gentiles could appear "clean" also? Apparently so! The king addressed the good guys first, and the logical flow was the same for both. Both the reward and punishment would be great at the judgment day with the inheritance of the kingdom at stake. Here is the logic of how the king would measure the two.

25:35 starts with the word "for," denoting the reason why the judgment would be cast in this way. Jesus stated that those who would be rewarded had been faithful in feeding, clothing, healing, and caring for Jesus himself in 25:35–36. Those who did would receive an inheritance (i.e., "eternal life" in 25.46b), and those who did not would receive the eternal fire reserved for the devil and his messengers (i.e., "eternal punishment" in 25:46a). Within this story of *lex telionis*, Jesus created a very telling dialogue among the characters. Jesus used the word "when" among the righteous in 25:37–39 to touch on a broader contextual question.

The biggest question is "when" at the beginning of this discourse at 24:3. This is a direct echo of that question. When will you come back, Lord? Jesus already stated the only thing they needed to do was to stay alert. This passage in 25:37–39 is another way to use "when" in relation to the deeds done by sheep and goats. Thus, Jesus used the "when" creatively in the beginning and the end of the long eschatological discourse. The important issue was neither when the Son of Man would come nor deliberately noting when a good deed was exclusively and intentionally done for the Son of Man. Instead, the most important issue was the righteous doing the normal righteous deeds, much like the faithful slaves of 24:45–51 and 25:14–30 as well as the wise virgins of 25:1–13.

The righteous work is the intentional work of kindness done with no intention of being rewarded. The surprise both the sheep and the goats expressed shows that works in this life have far greater impact, both positively and negatively, than imagined. In other words, Jesus' profound conclusion gives this message. Do not ask when the Son of Man would come, but treat people as if the Son of Man had come and was on the receiving end of good works. Treat the Son of Man as if he is here now.

In Jesus' society, his conclusion had radical implications. The oppressed poor had no power. They relied on the powerful patrons who would help them, often when the help would benefit the rich. Jesus would be the patron, if he really were the Son of Man. In an inconspicuous sense, the poor would now be the patrons because they unintentionally embodied the Son of Man. The power of the Son of Man was now realized in the powerless poor. Jesus created a most radical kingdom reversal of honor and shame.

In this final parable, Jesus had brought out several important themes of his teaching in the discourse through the three parables being rounded up by the present final parable. The first theme is alertness. The second theme relates to the first theme by further defining what alertness means. The second theme, then, is the identity of the disciple and the faith community. So long as the followers did their duty in accordance to their identity, they would land on the right side. The third theme progressively defined what duty would look like. Jesus clearly showed that duty included helping the oppressed. Yet, the personification of Jesus in the oppressed showed even a wider definition of duty. Duty meant to live intentional righteousness in this oppressive world system as if the Son of Man had already arrived so that every deed would be done as if it were done to the Son of Man. Matthew's Jesus had just provided a powerful metaphorical Christological ethic. This unique Christology was not mainly about ontology in systematic theological terminologies, but was mainly about ethical outworking of kingdom righteousness. Jesus had personified himself in the oppressed. Having proclaimed the basis of the eschatological standard, Jesus either had an overly inflated view of himself or he was the Christ.

Jesus would later declare his place as the eschatological Son of Man in his trial in 26:64 that had triggered further anger among the religious authority that led to his eventual death. For now, Jesus had identified with the powerless by making them powerful, not by exchanging places with them but by infusing their existence with Christological significance. All the righteous of the kingdom would identify with these powerless by seeing Christ's power in their poverty and oppression. At the same time, the disciples would also see their own places in later suffering for Christ (cf. 5:10). They themselves might end up being thrown into prison or living in poverty (24:9), and those who would stand firm with those under such pressure also would demonstrate their place in the kingdom. Thus, with one powerful Christological narrative, Jesus infused both the poor and the persecuted kingdom citizens with power. At the same time, Jesus obliged others to side with the poor rather than the powerful (cf. 10:40–42).[1] Picking the right side is goal of the lesson on alertness, identity, and personal responsibility in these eschatological parables.

We come back to the issue of sheep and goats now. We have already seen above that sheep and goats were ritually clean animals that resembled each other. Yet, judgment required the Son of Man to pick sheep over goats. Jesus' choice of animals shows how closely the two opposing parties resembled each other. Both were ritually clean. Jesus then was not talking about a contrast between believers and pagans or between Jews and gentiles.[2] Now, we should interpret this parable based on 24:42–44 to get the point about the usage of sheep and goats. Within the context of the temple, Jesus was using two similar animals to talk about the reality or appearance of religiosity. With the broader theme of righteousness in Matthew, we should note that Jesus compared righteousness done before others versus true righteousness of the kingdom (6:1). In the same way, the acts of righteousness stated in the parable by Jesus would also be done without deliberate knowledge of reward or accounting. Jesus was contrasting two seemingly pure groups, much like sheep and goats. This narrative makes perfect sense in the context of the temple. Jesus here distinguished two groups that were normally hard to distinguish ritualistically. Jesus did not want the appearance of piety, or ritual purity only, but wanted true religiosity in righteous work (cf. 6:1). Righteous work of the sheep was not contrived within a traditional religious framework (i.e., "Lord, when did we . . .") but existed in the way the righteous viewed the people of the world. The action resulting from their view inadvertently served Christ. Thus, Jesus did not only want to talk about righteous work, but also about appearance versus substance. On the contrary, the goats thought that they had done enough, thus asking Jesus when they failed to minister to Jesus. Such self-satisfaction would meet the harshest of eschatological judgment. Self-satisfaction is no trait for the truly pure and pious.

1. The section 10:40–42 strikes a strong parallel with the ethics here. There is no certainty that those who received either the disciples or the prophets or Jesus or the little ones knew that they were deliberately either serving Jesus or going for some kind of eschatological reward. Jesus was just stating a fact in 10:40–42.

2. After all, the judgment would be over "all the nations."

In my backward telling of the story, I seem to be talking only about the inclusiveness of the kingdom if both sheep and goats were allowed in. I also took out the Christological ethic in the teaching of Jesus, a most important explanation of the parable. Yet, when Jesus told his story, these elements were highly significant. With the sheep being separated from the kosher goats, Jesus' teaching declared clear separation not along the dividing lines of his day (i.e., Jews-gentiles, believers-pagans, etc.). In fact, both parties could talk to the "Lord" in the final judgment. The second party, the goats, resembled those who would say "Lord, Lord" in 7:21 and 25:11. Matthew's masterful usage of the exclamatory "Lord . . ." motif has reached its climax in this final discourse.

Jesus made clear the point that not everyone who called him "Lord" would be an heir of the kingdom. As if trying to preach one complete sermon with all his discourses, Matthew ended Jesus' introductory discourse with the "Lord, Lord" motif only to bring back the address to the "Lord" in the concluding part of the last discourse. The dominical motif surely points to Jesus' authority. Like a great sermon composed of a related introduction and conclusion, Matthew had successfully preached through Jesus' discourses from the introduction of the kingdom to the climax of the future kingdom. Is this parable not the most appropriate conclusion to all of Jesus' discourses?

PUTTING THE TEXT IN HISTORY: MEANINGS FOR THE WORLD OF AUTHOR-READERS

Matthew's community struggled not only with the destruction of the temple and its associated rituals, but also with the meaning of piety and identity. Thus, there were two layers of meaning for Matthew's audience. Even before the temple destruction, people argued over the definition of piety, evident in James 1:27. Within a community so steeped in rituals and rich traditions dating all the way back to the founding of Israel, Matthew's audience surely needed a handle on how Christ's coming had affected them.

The early church also debated the meaning of Jesus as the Son of Man. These were the beginning of the Christological debates that climaxed in the later Nicene Council in 325 CE. Whatever people thought about it, Matthew's answer was much more practical. His community was to become familiar with who they were. They were the alert community awaiting a future judgment of all humanity. Everyone who claimed to be a true Israelite was not necessarily one. Everyone who claimed to be follower of Jesus was not necessarily a follower. Matthew transferred the focus from rituals to good work. Matthew's recording of the eschatological discourse was his way of telling his community to look forward to doing some good rather than mourning over the lost temple. The community was to be the true heir of the kingdom by living out godly ethics under Jesus' lordship. Thus, Christological piety would be the first layer of meaning for Matthew's audience. The acts of kindness would mark the mission of the church as well as the alertness that would mark the true disciple.

For Matthew's audience, there was yet another layer of meaning within the parable that went beyond judgment to dealing with the community's identity. The Christomorphic description of the poor, naked, and oppressed also fit the experience of at least some members of Matthew's audience whose mission to "all the nations" (28:18–20) brought them alienation. They were hated "because of me" (cf. 24:9). As such, they embodied Jesus. The judgment here was based on how people treated the embodied community of Christ. In other words, the kingdom made a clear dividing point and judgment would not only be dependent on how the disciples treated the poor but also about how the world treated the oppressed disciples. The kingdom resisted neutrality. Therefore, if the community of Matthew were doing its duty but received unfair treatment, its members could take comfort in the fact that they too embodied Jesus Christ in their mission and justice would ultimately be on their side. The parable then served as encouragement for Matthew's audience to do good in spite of sometimes adverse circumstances. In summary, the church that suffered would also alleviate the suffering of this world.

A Christian professor was talking to a Jewish rabbi one day. The Christian professor asked, "Does my beard make me look like a rabbi?" The quick-witted rabbi answered, "No more than a goat having a goatee looks like a rabbi." We may get a chuckle out of this true story, but it illustrates perfectly what Jesus was talking about. Appearances can be deceiving.

Jesus' harsh conclusion has a lot of to say to the faith community today. Organized religion has the appearance of respectability. In some quarters, the faith community even appears morally superior (though not so in other quarters). Appearance is deceiving. Real piety and kingdom inheritance, according Matthew's Jesus, have nothing to do with appearance. Both sides appear to be religious, but the main issue for Jesus was whether the kingdom citizen lives life by serving those not normally noticed by society and organized religion. That is the main difference.

As I finish writing about this parable and wrapping up this book, something dramatic is happening in Hong Kong where I taught for a few years. One of the largest dockworkers strikes in recent years has paralyzed one of the most active free ports of the world. One example of the reason for the strikes is due to the low wages and long hours these people have had to endure. The average crane driver works daily twelve-hour shifts, sometimes with overtime adding up to eighteen-hour days. Their wages have decreased in large amount since the handover of 1997 from the British to the Chinese. The inflation of goods however has steadily increased above five percent every year and has only increased past six percent in the last few years. In other words, if these workers had maintained their wages in 1997, they would have still lost enormous amount of money, but to lose more wages would move them dangerously towards the poverty line. Meanwhile, the Beijing loyalist trade alliance union has said nothing. No one would stand up for these people, not the government and not even most churches—and definitely not most seminaries. In one of the statistics I looked at, Hong Kong ranks third in free port activity, below the number two Singapore and number one Shanghai. In other words, the companies involved have made a lot of money with voluminous goods exchanged, but somehow the money has not trickled down to those who helped build success. What does this have to do with the gospel and the parable Jesus just told? Let me continue my story.

At the same time the above events are unfolding, several mega-church pastors (whose names will be withheld here) have actively discouraged any kind of ecclesiastical social action against the oppressive government policy on the one hand and the greedy policy of corporations on the other, citing a few misinterpreted proof texts from Paul's letters (e.g., Romans 13). Based on Jesus' parable here, no matter how many verses the speaker quotes from the Bible, the message is no gospel of the kingdom.

While all this high-handed exercise of false proof text was going on in pulpits, I have a group of friends including some of my students who visit the strikers nightly to show spiritual and financial support. My group of friends is doing good to Jesus by serving the "least" in the society much more than this foreign mission that acts more like missiological imperialism rather than true kingdom work. People need to reflect on what the gospel mission really is because many have missed the boat. If we read the teachings of Matthew and Jesus in a straightforward manner, Jesus was not merely talking about preaching the gospel and getting conversion numbers.

He was talking about demonstrating the gospel in good works. Apparently, serving others has greater moral value to Jesus than popular Christian morality today.

There is something yet more profound going on in this parable here. People in Matthew's day treated king's with love and respect because there was so much advantage to be had from such a relationship. Once again, relationship was defined by power transaction in a patron-client society. People however did not treat the poor with much respect for none other than the lack of benefit in such a relationship. Jesus' value moves the opposite direction. Precisely, when the church befriend those least beneficial to her would she receive the most advantage and power. The power of the King resides not in the King Himself but through the powerless. The relevance for the present faith community is as undeniable today as it was then.

My above example will sound very uncomfortable. Jesus' parable was unsettling also, as he called out those who clearly and apparently knew his name. No wonder right after he finished all that he said, the religious leaders wanted to kill him (26:1–5). Preaching this parable and the other three previous parables has huge risks. Matthew's teachings through Jesus' mouth are radically unsettling. For preachers who want to preach pleasing and comfortable sermons, they must avoid these texts altogether. For those who love truth and possess courage, this text will challenge the church in a real and substantial way. Its radicalness needs to be brought out, or else this would be just another sermon that sounds like "Jesus will come back and judge but let's congratulate each other because we already know Jesus. Let's now tell others about Jesus and bring them to revival meetings." The following is the suggested format of the sermon.

Title: Deceiving Appearance
Telling It Backward: Sheep and goats are equally clean animals . . . but Jesus has a different way of looking at what is clean. What are the attitudes of those who would sit at the right hand and left hand of the king?

1) The Sheep: Serving Christ (25:34–40)
2) The Goats: Not Serving Christ (25:41–46)
Conclusion: The key is both sheep and goats look alike. We must know the difference, and then live by that knowledge.

REFLECTION QUESTIONS

1. How does the parable relate to the rest of the discourse?

2. Why is the usage of these two animals important for Jesus' argument?

3. What does the conversation about the attitudes of the sheep and the goats tell us?

4. What is it that the sheep got right?

5. How does the parable address Matthew's community?

6. What are some other examples in Matthew that would define the righteousness of the sheep?

7. What does this say about the gospel that the faith community believes today?

Bibliography

Bakhtin, Mikhail. *The Dialogic Imagination*. Translated by Caryl Emerson and Michael Holquist, edited by Michael Holquist. Austin: University of Texas, 1981.

Bauckham, Richard. "From Whom Were Gospels Written?" In *The Gospels for All Christians*, edited by Richard Bauckham, 9–48. Grand Rapids: Eerdmans, 1998.

Brosend, William. *Conversations with Scripture*. Harrisburg/New York: Morehouse, 2006.

Crossan, John Dominic. *The Power of Parable*. San Francisco: Harper One, 2012.

McLaren, James S. "A Reluctant Provincial," In *The Gospel of Matthew in its Roman Imperial Context*, edited by John Riches and David C. Sim, 34–48. London: T & T Clark, 2005.

Scheller, Christine A. "How Far Should Forgiveness Go? Seventy Times Seven? I can barely forgive some corrupt clergy once." *Christianity Today* 54/10 (2010): 40–44.

Snodgrass, Klyne R. *Stories with Intent*. Grand Rapids: Eerdmans, 2008.

Thompson, Michael B. "The Holy Internet." In *The Gospels for All Christians*, edited by Richard Bauckham, 49–70. Grand Rapids: Eerdmans, 1998.